Study Guide

for

Criminal Procedure for the Criminal Justice System

Study Guide

for

Criminal Procedure for the Criminal Justice System

Ninth Edition

John N. Ferdico

THOMSON
WADSWORTH

Australia • Canada • Mexico • Singapore • Spain • United Kingdom • United States

Printed in the United States of America
1 2 3 4 5 6 7 07 06 05 04

Printer: West Group

ISBN: 0-534-62920-2

For more information about our products,
contact us at:
Thomson Learning Academic Resource Center
1-800-423-0563

For permission to use material from this text,
contact us by:
Phone: 1-800-730-2214
Fax: 1-800-730-2215
Web: http://www.thomsonrights.com

Thomson Wadsworth
10 Davis Drive
Belmont, CA 94002-3098
USA

Asia
Thomson Learning
5 Shenton Way #01-01
UIC Building
Singapore 068808

Australia/New Zealand
Thomson Learning
102 Dodds Street
Southbank, Victoria 3006
Australia

Canada
Nelson
1120 Birchmount Road
Toronto, Ontario M1K 5G4
Canada

Europe/Middle East/South Africa
Thomson Learning
High Holborn House
50/51 Bedford Row
London WC1R 4LR
United Kingdom

Latin America
Thomson Learning
Seneca, 53
Colonia Polanco
11560 Mexico D.F.
Mexico

Spain/Portugal
Paraninfo
Calle/Magallanes, 25
28015 Madrid, Spain

TABLE OF CONTENTS

CHAPTER 1
FRAMEWORK FOR THE STUDY OF CRIMINAL PROCEDURE

KEY TERMS AND CONCEPTS

BAIL – An amount of money that the criminal defendant gives to the court to assure that he will show up in court on the date and time required.

BILL OF ATTAINDER – A legislative enactment that provides for an automatic penalty without a trial or hearing.

CIVIL RIGHTS – The privileges and freedoms that are accorded all Americans by virtue of their citizenship.

COLLATERAL ESTOPPEL DOCTRINE – an issue of ultimate fact that has been determined by a valid and final judgment cannot again be litigated between the same parties in any future lawsuit.

COMPULSORY PROCESS – guarantees the defendant's right to compel the attendance of favorable witnesses at trial, usually by means of a court-issued subpoena.

CONFRONTATION – guarantees the accused the right to confront hostile witnesses at his or her criminal trial.

CROSS EXAMINATION – the defendant's right to test both the witness's credibility and the witness's knowledge of relevant facts of the case.

DOUBLE JEOPARDY – The process of subjecting the criminal defendant to multiple trials or punishments for the same offense.

DUAL SOVEREIGNTY DOCTRINE – the doctrine preventing double jeopardy when a single act violates both federal and state laws and the defendant is exposed to prosecution in both federal and state courts.

DUE PROCESS OF LAW – The concept that government must follow established rules and procedures when taking away or limiting an individual's rights.

EQUAL PROTECTION OF THE LAWS - This requirement prevents any state from making unreasonable, arbitrary distinctions between different persons as to their rights and privileges.

***EX POST FACTO* LAW** – A retroactive criminal law. A criminal law enacted today that makes something you did in the past a crime and attempts to punish you for it.

FELONY – a crime for which a sentence of more than one year's imprisonment can be imposed.

HABEAS CORPUS – Petitioning for a writ of *habeas corpus* is the procedure by which a federal court is enlisted to inquire into alleged illegal detention and requested to issue an order directing authorities to release the petitioner.

HEARSAY EVIDENCE – a statement, other than one made by the declarant while testifying at the trial or hearing, offered in evidence to prove the truth of the matter asserted.

IMMUNITY – protects witnesses from use of their testimony and any evidence derived from the testimony in future prosecutions.

JUDICIAL REVIEW – The doctrine stating that it is the province of the courts to decide when laws are in violation of the Constitution and to declare those laws unconstitutional.

PROBABLE CAUSE – The amount of evidence necessary to obtain a search warrant or to justify an arrest. Knowledge of facts and circumstances that would allow a reasonable person to believe that a crime had been committed and that the property listed in the search warrant application was in the place listed or in an arrest that there was evidence of guilt that makes it more likely than not that the person committed the crime.

SUBPOENA - A document issued by a court that requires a person to come to court and testify as a witness.

TESTIMONIAL COMMUNICATIONS – a communication which, explicitly or implicitly, relate a factual assertion or disclose information.

TREASON – Giving aid and comfort to the enemy. Under the United States Constitution, two witnesses to an overt act or confession in open court are required for conviction.

WARRANT – a court order, requiring probable cause, authorizing search, seizure, and/or arrest of a citizen.

<u>KEY COURT CASES</u>

Marbury v. Madison (1803)

Twining v. New Jersey (1908)

Argersinger v. Hamlin (1972)

Gideon v. Wainwright (1963)

Coker v. Georgia (1977)

Gregg v. Georgia (1976)

Griswold v. Connecticut (1965)

CHAPTER OUTLINE

I. Introduction
- A. Conflicting governmental functions—balancing the function of maintaining law and order
    - i. Maintaining law and order
    - ii. Protecting rights of citizens

II. The Original Constitution
- A. Replaced Articles of Confederation
- B. Adopted by Continental Congress September 17, 1787
- C. Ratification by states
- D. Three branches of government established
    - i. Legislative
    - ii. Executive
    - iii. Judicial
- E. Balance of Powers
    - i. Judicial Review
    - ii. Marbury v. Madison (1803)
- F. Concern by the small states that new Constitution lacks an enumeration of citizens' rights

III. The Bill of Rights
- A. Ten Amendments to U. S. Constitution
- B. Added by Congress in 1789
- C. Ratification by states in 1791
- D. Limited powers of national government only
- E. Relationship of the 14th Amendment to the Bill of Rights
    - i. Applied Bill of Rights as restriction on state governments.
    - ii. "Total incorporation" approach
        1. 14th Amendment applies all of Bill of Rights to States
        2. This approach never adopted by Supreme Court
    - iii. "Fundamental rights" approach
      Saw fundamental rights springing from due process clause
        1. Used by Court to restrict state governments until about 1960
    - iv. "Selective incorporation" approach
        1. Bill of Rights applied to states on a case by case basis
        2. The Supreme Court under this approach has applied some, but not all, rights in the Bill of Rights to the states

IV. Individual Rights in the Constitution
- A. The privilege of the writ of *habeas corpus*

B. No bills of attainder
C. No *ex post facto* laws
D. Treason defined

V. Individual Rights in the Bill of Rights

A. First Amendment
   i. Freedom of religion
      1. Free exercise
      2. No denomination will be a state supported church
   ii. Freedom of Speech
   iii. Freedom of Press
   iv. Freedom of Assembly
B. Second Amendment
   i. Right to bear arms
C. Third Amendment
D. Fourth Amendment
   i. Prohibition on unreasonable searches and seizures
   ii. Search warrant requirements
E. Fifth Amendment
   i. Indictment by Grand Jury
   ii. Double jeopardy prohibited
   iii. Compelled self-incrimination prohibited
   iv. Due process of law required
   v. Eminent Domain requires just compensation
F. Sixth Amendment
   i. Right to a speedy and public trial
      1. Trial by impartial jury
   ii. Right to notice of charges
   iii. Right to confrontation with witnesses
   iv. Guarantee of compulsory process
   v. Right to representation by counsel
G. Seventh Amendment
H. Eighth Amendment
   i. Right to bail
   ii. Freedom from cruel and unusual punishment
I. Ninth Amendment
J. Tenth Amendment
K. Thirteenth Amendment
   i. Prohibition of slavery
L. Fourteenth Amendment
   i. Right to due process
   ii. Right to equal protection of the laws
M. Fifteenth Amendment
   i. Right to vote shall not be abridged or denied based on race, color, or prior servitude
N. Nineteenth Amendment
   i. Right to vote shall not be abridged or denied based on sex

O. Twenty-sixth Amendment
    i. Right to vote at age eighteen
P. Twenty-fourth Amendment
    i. Right to vote shall not be abridged or denied based on failure to pay a tax

REVIEW QUESTIONS

Fill in the blank:

1. Before the Constitution was adopted, the United States government functioned under a document called the ____________________.

2. The first ten Amendments to the United States Constitution are collectively called the ____________________________.

3. The U. S. Supreme Court decision that established the authority of the Supreme Court to rule on the constitutionality of acts of Congress was ____________________.

4. Under the United States Constitution, the branch of government that enacts the laws is called the ____________________.

5. Under the United States Constitution, the branch of government that enforces the laws is called the ______________________.

6. Under the United States Constitution, the branch of government that interprets the laws is called the _______________________.

7. A legislative enactment that provides for an automatic penalty without a trial or hearing is called a(n)_______________________.

8. A retroactive criminal law is called a(n)____________________________.

9. In the United States Constitution, Article III deals with the ____________________.

10. A person who commits an overt act that gives aid to the enemy during time of war would be guilty of ________________________.

11. The United States Constitution, in the _______________Amendment, guarantees freedom of religion.

12. The right of citizens to assemble to peacefully petition their government is guaranteed by the __________________ Amendment to the United States Constitution.

13. The right to be represented in a criminal trial by an attorney is guaranteed in the ________________ Amendment to the United States Constitution.

14. Cruel and unusual punishments are prohibited by the ________________ Amendment to the United States Constitution.

15. The Amendment to the United States Constitution that is used to impose upon the states the restrictions guaranteed in the U.S. Constitution is the ________________ Amendment.

16. The right of a criminal defendant to confront the witnesses against them at trial is guaranteed by the ________________ Amendment to the United States Constitution.

17. The United States Supreme Court case that guaranteed indigent defendants in felony trials the right to a court appointed attorney was ______________________________.

18. The right to equal protection of the laws is contained in the ______________ Amendment to the United States Constitution.

19. Excessive bail is prohibited by the _______________ Amendment to the United States Constitution.

20. Compelled self-incrimination is prohibited by the _____________ Amendment to the United States Constitution.

True or False:

1. _____The Bill of Rights was part of the United States Constitution when it was first written and proposed to the states.

2. _____The concept of "total incorporation," in which the Fourteenth Amendment to the United States Constitution would have applied the entire Bill of Rights to the states, was never adopted by a majority of the United States Supreme Court.

3. _____The approach used by the courts to apply the Bill of Rights to the states today is called "selective incorporation."

4. _____The courts have applied all of the rights guaranteed under the Bill of Rights to the states under the Fourteenth Amendment.

5. _____To increase judicial efficiency, the United States Constitution allows for criminal penalties to be assessed without a trial or hearing.

6. _____Due process of law is guaranteed by the Fifth Amendment to the United States Constitution.

7. _____An attempt by Congress to establish a national religion in the United States would be contrary to the First Amendment to the United States Constitution.

8. _____“Symbolic speech” is protected by the First Amendment to the United States Constitution.

9. _____The right to bear arms is protected by the Second Amendment to the United States Constitution.

10. _____Protection from unreasonable searches and seizures is contained in the Fourth Amendment to the United States Constitution.

11. _____The prohibition against double jeopardy does not apply if the offense violates both state and federal laws.

12. _____The prohibition on compelled self-incrimination prohibits confessions by persons accused of a crime.

13. _____Eminent domain involves the government taking private property for public use.

14. _____The Sixth Amendment to the United States Constitution requires that the criminal defendant be advised of the charges against them.

15. _____To prevail on appeal on the basis of ineffective assistance of counsel, a criminal defendant need only show that his trial attorney’s performance fell below the objective standard of reasonableness.

16. _____Bail is assessed against a criminal defendant to punish him for his actions.

17. _____The Eighth Amendment to the United States Constitution requires that the penalty be proportional to the crime committed.

18. _____The United States Supreme Court has interpreted the Bill of Rights to include a right of privacy.

19. _____The Thirteenth Amendment to the United States Constitution prohibits slavery.

20. _____Poll taxes that must be paid before you can vote are constitutional under the United States Constitution.

21. _____A prosecutor can compel a witness to testify at trial if they give their immunity.

22. _____A person is entitled to the assistance of counsel at all critical stages of a criminal prosecution.

23. _____The right to a speedy trial is guaranteed in the Sixth Amendment to the United States Constitution.

24. _____The rights guaranteed by the United States Constitution are absolute and cannot be limited or restricted in any manner whatsoever.

Multiple Choice:

1. The Amendment to the United States Constitution that prohibits excessive bail is the:
   A. First
   B. Second
   C. Fourth
   D. Fifth
   E. Eighth

2. The Amendment to the United States Constitution that provides for the right to have an attorney at a criminal trial is the:
   A. First
   B. Second
   C. Fourth
   D. Fifth
   E. Sixth

3. The United States Supreme Court case that stated that the right of an indigent criminal defendant to have a court appointed attorney if charged with a felony was:
   A. Marbury v. Madison
   B. Griswold v. Connecticut
   C. Gideon v. Wainwright
   D. Murphy v. Minnesota
   E. Robinson v. California

4. Freedom of the press is guaranteed by which amendment to the United States Constitution?
   A. First
   B. Second
   C. Third
   D. Fourth
   E. Sixth

5. The Amendment to the United States Constitution that prohibits unreasonable searches and seizures is the:
   A. First
   B. Second
   C. Fourth
   D. Fifth
   E. Sixth

6. The Amendment to the United States Constitution that prohibits double jeopardy is the:

A. First
B. Second
C. Fourth
D. Fifth
E. Sixth

7. The right to bear arms is contained in which amendment to the United States Constitution?

A. First
B. Second
C. Fifth
D. Eighth
E. Ninth

8. The amendment that guarantees the right to a speedy and public trial is the:

A. Fourth
B. Fifth
C. Sixth
D. Eighth
E. Ninth

9. The Amendment to the United States Constitution that guarantees freedom of speech is the:

A. First
B. Second
C. Fourth
D. Fifth
E. Sixth

10. The amendment to the United States Constitution that prohibits double jeopardy is the:

A. Fourth
B. Fifth
C. Sixth
D. Eighth
E. Ninth

11. The amendment to the United States Constitution that has been used by the courts to apply the Bill of Rights to the states is the:

A. First
B. Fourth
C. Sixth
D. Eighth
E. Fourteenth

12. The legal theory that says that once an issue of ultimate fact has been fully decided in one case the issue cannot be re-litigated in another case involving the same parties is called:
    - *A. Ex post facto*
    - B. Bill of Attainder
    - C. Double Jeopardy
    - D. Collateral Estoppel
    - *E. Res Ipse Locquitor*

13. The Amendment to the United States Constitution that prohibits compelled self-incrimination is the:
    - A. Fourth
    - B. Fifth
    - C. Sixth
    - D. Eighth
    - E. Fourteenth

14. The Amendment to the United States Constitution that guarantees a right to a trial by jury is the:
    - A. First
    - B. Fourth
    - C. Fifth
    - D. Sixth
    - E. Eighth

15. The Amendment to the United States Constitution that provides for a right for the criminal defendant to be confronted by the witnesses against him is the:
    - A. Fourth
    - B. Fifth
    - C. Sixth
    - D. Eighth
    - E. Fourteenth

16. The Amendment to the United States Constitution that prohibits cruel and unusual punishments is the:
    - A. Fourth
    - B. Fifth
    - C. Sixth
    - D. Eighth
    - E. Fourteenth

17. The Amendment to the United States Constitution that gives a criminal defendant the right to cross examination of the prosecution's witnesses is the:

A. Fourth
B. Fifth
C. Sixth
D. Eighth
E. Fourteenth

18. The Amendment to the United States Constitution that guarantees a criminal defendant the right to appeal a conviction is the:

A. Fourth
B. Fifth
C. Sixth
D. Eighth
E. Ninth

19. The decision of the United States Supreme Court that held that a criminal defendant charged with a misdemeanor could not be sentenced to jail unless they had been represented at trial by an attorney was:

A. Argersinger v. Hamlin
B. Marbury v. Madison
C. Coker v. Georgia
D. Griswold v. Connecticut
E. Malloy v. Hogan

20. The decision of the United States Supreme Court that held that "total incorporation" was the wrong approach for determining which of the rights guaranteed by the Bill of Rights were applicable against the states was:

A. Marbury v. Madison
B. Coker v. Georgia
C. Gideon v. Wainwright
D. Twining v. New Jersey
E. Ohio v. Johnson

21. Under the United States Constitution, the right to due process is guaranteed by the:

A. Fourth Amendment
B. Fifth Amendment
C. Sixth Amendment
D. Fourteenth Amendment
E. Both the Fifth and the Fourteenth Amendments

22. The United States Supreme Court decision that suggested that citizens have a right of privacy that flows from the Bill of Rights was:
    A. Griswold v. Connecticut
    B. Gideon v. Wainwright
    C. Argersinger v. Hamlin
    D. Twining v. New Jersey
    E. Mapp v. Ohio

23. The Amendment to the United States Constitution that protects citizens from the state's making unreasonable and arbitrary distinctions among different people as to their rights and privileges is the:
    A. First
    B. Fourth
    C. Fifth
    D. Ninth
    E. Fourteenth

Essay Questions:

1. Which of the Amendments to the United States Constitution is the most important? Why?

2. Why were some of the states reluctant to ratify the United States Constitution until a Bill of Rights was added?

3. Why is an *ex post facto* law unfair?

4. The right to bear arms guaranteed by the Second Amendment to the United States Constitution is not absolute. What restrictions have the legislatures put on the right to possess firearms?

5. The Constitution guarantees freedom of speech, but even that right has some limitations. What limitations are there on freedom of speech?

CHAPTER 2
CRIMINAL COURTS AND CRIMINAL TRIALS

KEY TERMS AND CONCEPTS

ACQUITTAL – Judgment which finds that the evidence presented has not proven guilty beyond a reasonable doubt.

AFFIDAVIT – A document that contains a statement by a person who has sworn under oath that the statement is true to the best of his knowledge and belief.

APPEAL – One of two major avenues of relief after a defendant has been convicted of a crime.

APPELLATE JURISDICTION – The authority to deal with a case only after it has been finally decided by a lower court of original jurisdiction, and then only to revise or correct the proceedings of the lower court.

ARRAIGNMENT – An appearance before a judge by a person under indictment where the defendant is advised of the charges against him and asked to enter a plea to those charges.

BAIL – An amount of money that the criminal defendant gives to the court to assure that he will show up in court on the date and time required.

BENCH TRIAL – A trial where there is a judge, but no jury.

BILL OF PARTICULARS – A document giving the accused specific details of the charges made by the prosecutor.

BURDEN OF PROOF – The requirement in a criminal trial that the prosecution must meet for a defendant to be found guilty.

CHALLENGE FOR CAUSE – A means to have a prospective juror dismissed during *voir dire* which is directed toward the qualifications of a juror.

COMPLAINT – A document outlining the facts and circumstances that lead the person signing the complaint to believe that the person listed in the complaint has committed a crime. The complaint forms the basis for issuance of an arrest warrant.

COURTS OF GENERAL JURSIDICTION – a court whose trial jurisdiction either includes no felonies or is limited to less than all felonies and that may or may not hear appeals.

COURTS OF LIMITED JURSIDICTION – A court of limited jurisdiction is limited to a particular class or classes of cases.

CROSS EXAMINATION – The right of defense counsel to question the prosecutions witness after the prosecution is through.

DEPOSITION – Taking the out-of-court testimony of a witness and preserving that testimony in writing for later use in court.

DIRECT EXAMINATION – The first examination of a witness.
DISCOVERY – Also called pretrial discovery, is a procedure, largely governed by statute or court rule, whereby the defendant or the prosecution is enabled to inspect, examine, copy, or photograph items in the possession of the other party.

DUPLICITOUS INDICTMENT – An indictment that unites two or more separate and distinct offenses in the same count.

FELONY – a crime for which a sentence of more than one year's imprisonment can be imposed.

GRAND JURY – The primary duty of the grand jury is to receive complaints in criminal cases, hear the evidence put forth by the state, and return an indictment when the jury is satisfied that there is probable cause that the defendant has committed an offense. The concurrence of a specified number of grand jurors is required to return an indictment.

HABEAS CORPUS – Petitioning for a writ of *habeas corpus* is the procedure by which a federal court is enlisted to inquire into alleged illegal detention and requested to issue an order directing authorities to release the petitioner.

HUNG JURY – When jurors are so irreconcilably divided in opinion that they are unable to agree on a verdict.

IMMUNITY – Protects witnesses from use of their testimony and any evidence derived from the testimony in future prosecutions.

INDICTMENT – In felony cases the document that charges the defendant with an offense and on which the defendant is brought to trial, returned by a grand jury and signed by the foreperson of the grand jury and the prosecuting attorney.

INFORMATION – In felony cases the document that charges the defendant with an offense and on which the defendant is brought to trial, signed only by the prosecuting attorney.

INSTRUCTIONS - Instructions given by the judge to the jury at the end of the trial just before they begin their deliberations. These instructions outline the duties of the jury and the law that is applicable to this case.

JUDGMENT – The written evidence of the final disposition of the case, signed by the judge.

JURISDICTION – The authority of a court to hear a particular type of case.

JURY NULLIFICATION – The power of a jury to acquit regardless of the strength of the evidence against a defendant.

JURY PANEL – A list of members of the community who are eligible for jury service.

MAGISTRATE - A judicial officer authorized to issue process in criminal cases.

MISDEMEANOR – A crime for which the maximum possible sentence is less than one year's imprisonment.

MOTION – A written or verbal request to a court asking the court to take some action.
MULTIPLICITOUS INDICTMENT – An indictment that charges the commission of a single offense in several counts.

NOLO CONTENDERE – A plea in which a defendant does not wish to contest the charges but does not wish to admit guilt. A *nolo contendere* plea can not be used against the defendant in a civil action.

NONJURY TRIAL – A trial without a jury.

ORIGINAL JURISDICTION – The authority to deal with a case from its beginning, including trying the case and passing judgment on the facts and the law.

PEREMPTORY CHALLENGE – A means to have a prospective juror dismissed during *voir dire* which requires no reason but is limited in number.

PRELIMINARY HEARING – A hearing at which the magistrate must determine whether there is probable cause to believe that an offense was committed and that the defendant committed it.

***PRIMA FACIE* CASE** – An objection to a peremptory challenge claiming discrimination.

PROBATION – A procedure by which a person found guilty of an offense is released by the court, subject to conditions imposed by the court, without being committed to a penal or correctional institution.

REASONABLE DOUBT – Proof beyond a reasonable doubt requires that the guilt of the defendant be established to a reasonable, but not absolute or mathematical, certainty.

REDIRECT EXAMINATION – The opportunity for the prosecution to re-examine a witness after the witness has been examined by the defense in order to rehabilitate the witness in the eyes of the jury.

SELECTIVE PROSECUTION – Selective prosecution is a violation of the equal protection clause of the Constitution. To establish selective prosecution, a defendant bears a heavy burden to show that others similarly situated were not prosecuted and that the defendant's prosecution was "deliberately based upon an unjustifiable standard such as race, religion, or other arbitrary classification." *Bordenkircher v. Hayes*, 434 U.S. 357, 364 (1978).

SUBPOENA – The process used to secure the attendance of witnesses or the production of books, papers, documents, or other objects at a criminal proceeding.

TRIAL *DE NOVO* – A new trial or retrial in which the whole case is examined again as if no trial had ever been held in the court of limited jurisdiction.

VENUE – The law holds that a criminal defendant's trial should be held in the geographical area where the crime was alleged to have been committed. A court's venue is the geographical area over which it has responsibility. The prosecution must show that the crime occurred within a court's geographical area in order for that court to hear the case.

VERDICT – the decision of the jury as to the defendant's guilt or innocence.

VINDICTIVE PROSECUTION – Vindictive prosecution violates due process. Vindictive prosecution occurs when a prosecutor increases the number or severity of charges to penalize a defendant who exercises constitutional or statutory rights.

VOIR DIRE – The examination of prospective jurors on the panel.

WRIT OF *CERTIORARI* – The Court, upon petition of a party, agrees to review a case decided by one of the circuit courts of appeals or the highest court of a state.

KEY CASES

Batson v. Kentucky (1986)

Brady v. Maryland (1963)

OUTLINE

I. Structure of the court system
- A. Federal courts
- B. State courts

II. Preliminary proceedings
- A. The complaint
- B. Affidavits
- C. Warrant or summons issues on the complaint
- D. Initial appearance

E. Preliminary Examination

III. Indictment and Information
   A. Sufficiency of indictment
   B. Joinder and severance
   C. Duplicity and multiplicity
   D. Prosecutorial discretion
   E. Grand jury
   F. Warrant or summons issued on the indictment

IV. Arraignment and preparation for trial
   A. Pleas
   B. Plea bargaining
   C. Motions
   D. Depositions
   E. Discovery
   F. Subpoena
   G. Competency to stand trial

V. Venue

VI. The trial
   A. Trial without a jury
   B. Trial with a jury
   C. Selection of jurors
   D. Jury composition
   E. Presentation of evidence
   F. Rules of evidence
   G. Order of presentation of evidence
   H. Motion for acquittal
   I. The defendant's evidence
   J. Rebuttal by the prosecution
   K. Closing arguments
   L. Instructions to the jury
   M. Verdict

VII. Sentence and judgment

VIII, Post trial motions

IX. Remedies after convictions
   A. Appeal
   B. Habeas Corpus
      a. State prisoners
      b. Federal prisoners
      c. State post conviction relief

REVIEW QUESTIONS

Fill in the blank:

1. In the federal court system, the trial court is called the ________________________.

2. In the federal court system, the intermediate court of appeals is called the

__________________________________.

3. In the federal system, the highest court is called the ______________________________.

4. A state court whose authority to hear cases is limited to misdemeanors and traffic offenses is called a court of __________________________________.

5. The legal document that is the basis for the issuance of an arrest warrant is called a(n)______________________.

6. A document that contains a statement made under oath and signed by the person making the statement is called a/an ______________________________.

7. Once a person is arrested they are brought before a judge without unnecessary delay for a/an __________________________________.

8. The purpose of a preliminary examination (preliminary hearing) is for the judge to determine if there is __________________________.

9. Knowledge of facts and circumstances that would lead a reasonable person to believe that a crime has been committed and that the defendant probably did it is called

________________________________.

10. In felony cases, the ____________________________ is the document that formally charges the defendant with the crime.

11. Indictments are issued after hearing the prosecution's presentation of the evidence in a felony case by the ____________________________.

12. A trial without a jury and only a judge is called a(n)______________________________.

13. A multiplicitous indictment is one that charges the defendant with more than one

_________________________.

14. A duplicitous indictment is one that charges the defendant with more than one

_______________________________.

15. The prosecutor's authority to determine who gets charged with a crime and what crime they will be charged with is known as ___________________________.

16. A plea that admits the act but contends that the act does not constitute a crime is called a plea of ______________________________.

17. Disposition of the criminal charges by agreement between the prosecution and defense before trial is called __________________________________.

18. An oral or written request to a court to issue a specified finding, decision or order is called a ______________________.

19. The process whereby the prosecution gives to the defendant copies of all reports, records and documents that will be used at trial against them is called ________________________________.

20. The United States Supreme Court case that prohibits peremptory challenges of jurors based upon race was ____________________________________.

True or False:

1. _____Before sentencing, a judge may permit a criminal defendant to withdraw his plea of guilty.

2. _____In some jurisdictions, an alternative to a Grand Jury indictment is an information.

3. _____In the federal court system, the trial court is the District Court.

4. _____The United States Supreme Court has nine judges.

5. _____All cases that are appealed from the Circuit Courts of Appeals are automatically heard by the United States Supreme Court.

6. _____The court systems in all of the states of the United States are set up exactly the same.

7. _____State courts of general jurisdiction have authority to hear all criminal cases within a county or geographical district.

8. _____In some cases, an arrest can be made without an arrest warrant.

9. _____The preliminary examination and the preliminary hearing are two names for the same thing.

10. _____Indictments are issued by a Grand Jury.

11. _____To prove that their prosecution was a case of "selective prosecution," a criminal defendant must prove that others similarly situated were not prosecuted, and that their prosecution was based on an unjustifiable standard such as race, religion or other arbitrary classification.

12. _____Grand Jury proceedings are traditionally held in secret.

13. _____In some jurisdictions, a criminal defendant may waive the right to a Grand Jury indictment and proceed to trial on an information.

14. _____To plead guilty or *nolo contendere*, the defendant must have the court's consent.

15. _____With regard to plea-bargaining, plea agreements are treated like contracts.

16. _____Under the United States Supreme Court decision in Brady v. Maryland, prosecutors have a continuing duty to advise the criminal defendant of any evidence they have that tends to show the innocence of the defendant.

17. _____"Incompetent to stand trial" and "not guilty by reason of insanity" are the same thing.

18. _____A trial without a jury is called a bench trial.

19. _____An attorney can use a peremptory challenge to remove a prospective juror for any reason whatsoever.

20. Jury instructions are given to the jury by the prosecutor.

Multiple Choice:

1. In a criminal case, sentencing is done by the:
    A. Jury
    B. Prosecutor
    C. Judge
    D. Defense attorney
    E. Victim of the crime

2. In a bench trial, questions of fact are decided by the:
    A. Jury
    B. Judge
    C. Bailiff
    D. Court clerk
    E. Prosecutor

3. The standard of proof necessary to convict in a criminal trial is:
    A. Suspicion of guilt
    B. Probable cause
    C. Proof beyond a reasonable doubt
    D. Clear and convincing evidence
    E. Absolute proof of guilt

4. In the federal court system, the intermediate appeals court is called the:
   A. District Court
   B. Superior Court
   C. Circuit Court of Appeals
   D. Supreme Court
   E. Court of Appellate Review

5. Immediately after arrest, a defendant is brought before a judge for a hearing called a:
   A. Trial
   B. Preliminary hearing
   C. Initial appearance
   D. Sentencing hearing
   E. Motion hearing

6. The amount of proof necessary to make a valid arrest is:
   A. Suspicion
   B. Proof beyond a reasonable doubt
   C. Preponderance of the evidence
   D. Clear and convincing evidence
   E. Probable cause

7. A document that is used as an alternative to an indictment is called a(n):
   A. Complaint
   B. Summons
   C. *Capias*
   D. Information
   E. True bill

8. Indictments are issued by:
   A. Judges
   B. Prosecutors
   C. Police officers
   D. Trial juries
   E. Grand juries

9. A document that charges a criminal defendant with two or more separate and distinct offenses is called a:
   A. Duplicitous indictment
   B. Multiplicitous indictment
   C. *Habeas Corpus*
   D. Collateral estoppel
   E. Plea bargain

10. The Amendment to the United States Constitution that provides for the grand jury process is the:
    A. First
    B. Second
    C. Fourth
    D. Fifth
    E. Sixth

11. The United States Supreme Court decision that requires prosecutors to turn over any evidence they have that tends to show the innocence of the defendant is:
    A. Gideon v. Wainwright
    B. Batson v. Kentucky
    C. Brady v. Maryland
    D. Santobello v. New York
    E. United States v. Calandra

12. The out of court testimony of a witness taken under oath is called a(n):
    A. Deposition
    B. Cross Examination
    C. Hearsay
    D. Indictment
    E. Bill of attainder

13. The United States Supreme Court decision that prohibits peremptory challenges of prospective jurors based on race was:
    A. Brady v. Maryland
    B. Gideon v. Wainwright
    C. Powell v. Ohio
    D. Batson v. Kentucky
    E. Mapp v. Ohio

14. In a jury trial, issues of law are decided by the:
    A. Judge
    B. Jury
    C. Prosecutor
    D. Clerk of Courts
    E. Defense attorney

15. The examination of prospective jurors to determine their fitness for jury service is called:
    A. Habeas corpus
    B. Indictment
    C. Impeachment
    D. Voir dire
    E. Collateral estoppel

16. The defense's motion for acquittal is made:
   A. Before trial
   B. After jury selection
   C. After the prosecution's presentation of evidence
   D. After the defense's presentation of evidence
   E. After the jury has begun deliberations

17. A person found guilty of a crime who is released by the judge to go back into the community under supervision instead of being incarcerated is said to be:
   A. On parole
   B. Under disability
   C. On probation
   D. Out on bail
   E. On furlough

18. Which of the following usually does **not** occur during the defendant's initial appearance before a judge?
   A. Judge advises defendant of the charges
   B. Bail is set by the judge
   C. Judge inquires if defendant is indigent
   D. Defendant enters a plea
   E. Judge inquires if defendant is represented by counsel

19. In the federal court system the highest appellate court, or the court of last resort, is the:
   A. Superior Court
   B. Appeals Court
   C. District Court
   D. Circuit Court of Appeals
   E. United States Supreme Court

20. The document issued by the United States Supreme Court that exercises its decision to hear a case on appeal is called a(n):
   A. Writ of *Habeas Corpus*
   B. Writ of Assistance
   C. Writ of Appeal
   D. Writ of *Certiorari*
   E. Writ of Prohibition

Essay Questions:

1. Recent decisions prohibit excluding prospective jurors because of race or gender. Are there other factors that should be included in this list? Why?

2. Why would a criminal defendant waive his right to a grand jury indictment?

3. What are the grounds for a successful appeal based on ineffective assistance of counsel?

4. Martin is accused of a heinous crime that he did not commit. Details of the gruesome crime are known throughout the community. Martin is certain that there is not sufficient evidence to convict him of the terrible crime. Why would Martin waive his right to a jury trial and opt for a bench trial?

5. In order to appeal their conviction based on an error made by the judge at trial, the rules require that the defendant (through their attorney) must have made an objection to the court at the time the error was made. What is the reason for this rule?

CHAPTER 3
BASIC UNDERLYING CONCEPTS

KEY TERMS AND CONCEPTS

ADMISSION – A voluntary acknowledgement of the existence of certain facts. An admission is not limited to words, but can include demeanor, conduct and acts of the person.

ATTENUATION DOCTRINE – This doctrine states that, even where the tainted evidence would not have been discovered except through the constitutional violation, there being no independent source, the evidence may still be admissible if the means of obtaining the evidence were sufficiently remote from and distinguishable from the primary illegality.

CORROBORATION – support with evidence or authority.

DERIVATIVE EVIDENCE – Evidence indirectly obtained as a result of other evidence.

EXCLUSIONARY RULE – A rule of evidence that prohibits the admission of illegally seized evidence at trial against the defendant.

FRUIT OF THE POISONOUS TREE DOCTRINE – A rule of evidence that holds that evidence that is derived from illegally seized evidence is also inadmissible at trial against the defendant.

GOOD-FAITH EXCEPTION - Under this exception, whenever a law enforcement officer acting with objective good faith has obtained a search warrant from a detached and neutral judge or magistrate and has acted within its scope, evidence seized pursuant to the warrant will not be excluded, even though the warrant is later determined to be invalid.

INDEPENDENT SOURCE DOCTRINE – This exception allows the admission of tainted evidence if that evidence was also obtained through a source wholly independent of the primary constitutional violation.

INEVITABLE DISCOVERY – An exception to the exclusionary rule that says that illegally seized evidence can be admitted if it would have been discovered by the police eventually anyway.

INFORMANT – Any person from whom a law enforcement officer obtains information on criminal activity.

PRIVACY – The right to freedom from unreasonable government intrusion.

PROBABLE CAUSE – The amount of evidence necessary to obtain a search warrant. Knowledge of facts and circumstances that would lead a reasonable person to believe that the items listed in an application for a search warrant are more likely than not at the place listed in the search warrant application.

REASONABLENESS – A flexible standard to be liberally construed for the protection of individual freedom.

SEARCH – A government action where an expectation of privacy that society is prepared to consider reasonable has been infringed.

SEIZURE – When some meaningful interference with an individual's possessory interest in property occurs.

STANDING – A defendant has standing when his or her own constitutional rights have been allegedly violated.

KEY CASES

Aguilar v. Texas (1964)

Brinegar v. United States (1949)

Carroll v. United States (1925)

Illinois v. Gates (1983)

Mapp v. Ohio (1961)

Nix v. Williams (1984)

Katz v. United States (1976)

Spinelli v. United States (1969)

United States v. Di Re (1948)

United States v. Leon (1984)

Weeks v. United States (1914)

Wong Sun v. United States (1963)

OUTLINE

I. The Exclusionary Rule
- A. Alternatives to the rule
- B. Federal-state conflict
- C. Criticism of the rule
- D. Fruit of the poisonous tree doctrine
  - a. Independent source
  - b. Attenuation
  - c. Inevitable discovery
- E. Good faith exception
- F. Standing requirement

II. Privacy

III. Probable Cause

IV. Reasonableness

REVIEW QUESTIONS

Fill in the blank:

1. The United States Supreme Court decision that applied the exclusionary rule to federal law enforcement officers in 1914 is ____________________.

2. The United States Supreme Court decision that applied the exclusionary rule to the states and local law enforcement officers is ______________________________.

3. The practice of state courts affording the accused greater protections under state law than that required by the United States Constitution is sometimes called the
________________________.

4. The ultimate authority of the interpretation of state law and the state's constitution is not the United States Supreme Court but the state's _________________________.

5. Evidence that is seized illegally is not ______________________ in court against the defendant in a criminal trial.

6. Derivative evidence is evidence that is found as a direct result of previously illegally seized _____________________.

7. Evidence that was obtained as a result of illegal seizure may be admissible if it was obtained through a source that was wholly _________________________ of the primary constitutional violation.

8. The exclusionary rule prohibits illegally seized evidence from being used against a defendant in a _____________________ trial.

9. The amendment to the United States Constitution that is involved with the exclusionary rule is the ____________ Amendment.

10. The exclusionary rule was designed to discourage misconduct by the _______________.

11. Police officers acting under the color of state law who violate a person's rights are subject to ____________________ for damages under federal law.

12. If sued, officers are entitled to a defense based on good faith that would provide them with qualified _______________________ from suits for money damages.

13. A person in a particular state may have rights under the state _________________ that exceed those available to them under the United States Constitution.

14. The United States Supreme Court case that established the inevitable discovery exception to the exclusionary rule was _____________________________.

15. The United States Supreme Court case that established the "good faith" exception to the exclusionary rule, where officers search under a search warrant later declared to be invalid, is _____________________________.

16. The "good faith" exception to the exclusionary rule reinforces the courts' preference for police searches conducted under the authority of a _____________________.

17. Unless a statute is clearly _______________________, a police officer can rely on that statute when conducting a search expressly authorized by the statute.

18. The exclusionary rule is not a bar to prosecution if the police have sufficient legally obtained _____________________ necessary to convict the defendant.

19. The United States Supreme Court decision in Katz v. the United States held that the Fourth Amendment protects _______________________, not places, from unreasonable searches and seizures.

20. Under the Fourth Amendment to the United States Constitution, a search or seizure must be _______________________.

True or False:

1. _____The exclusionary rule does not apply to actions by private persons.

2. _____The exclusionary rule is expressly written into the Fourth Amendment to the United States Constitution.

3. _____The exclusionary rule applied to federal law enforcement officers before it was applied to the states and local law enforcement officers.

4. _____The exclusionary rule is a rule of evidence established by the courts.

5. _____There are no exceptions to the exclusionary rule.

6. _____In Mapp. V. Ohio, the United States Supreme Court determined that the exclusionary rule should apply to local law enforcement officers.

7. _____A violation of the exclusionary rule is a bar to any prosecution of the defendant.

8. _____The "good faith" exception applies to all police searches and makes the exclusionary rule null and void.

9. _____Independent acts by private citizens seizing evidence are not covered by the exclusionary rule.

10. _____If a private citizen acts as an agent of the police and seizes evidence because of their direction, the exclusionary rule would apply.

11. _____The exclusionary rule applies only to evidence in criminal cases.

12. _____In order to object to an illegal search, the courts require that the person have some legal relationship to the property searched.

13. _____The right to privacy is expressly listed in the United States Constitution.

14. _____In order to obtain a search warrant, a police officer must have only suspicion to believe that the property listed in the search warrant application is in the place listed.

15. _____In a search warrant, both the place to be searched and the things or persons to be seized must be described with particularity.

16. _____In order to obtain a search warrant, police officers must be absolutely certain that the property they plan to seize is in the place listed on the search warrant application.

17. _____Search warrants are issued by judges.

18. _____Some searches can lawfully be conducted without a search warrant.

19. _____The Fourth Amendment to the United States Constitution prohibits unreasonable searches and seizures.

20. _____The exclusionary rule was designed to discourage police misconduct.

Multiple choice:

1. The Amendment to the United States Constitution that governs searches and seizures is the:
    A. First
    B. Fourth
    C. Fifth
    D. Sixth
    E. Eighth

2. The case that applied the exclusionary rule to the states and to local law enforcement officers was:
    A. Weeks v. United States
    B. Gideon v. Wainwright
    C. Mapp v. Ohio
    D. Nix v. Williams
    E. Miranda v. Arizona

3. Concerning the exclusionary rule, it can be said that:
    A. It existed before there was a United States Constitution
    B. It was part of the original United States Constitution
    C. It was added to the Constitution by the Bill of Rights
    D. It was adopted in a statute passed by Congress
    E. It is a rule of evidence adopted by the United States Supreme Court

4. The primary purpose of the exclusionary rule is to:
    A. Make police work difficult
    B. Allow defendants to escape punishment because of technicalities
    C. Provide the basis for appeal after conviction
    D. Discourage police misconduct
    E. Encourage plea bargaining

5. Officer Martin believes that Oscar is dealing drugs. Without a search warrant, Officer Martin goes to Oscar's house and forces his way into the house. In the living room, he finds cocaine. If introduced at trial against Oscar, the cocaine will most likely be:
    A. Admitted into evidence because possession of cocaine is illegal
    B. Admitted into evidence because Officer Martin really believed that Oscar was a drug dealer
    C. Admitted if Officer Martin did not break into Oscar's house but came through an unlocked door instead
    D. Suppressed because the search was unlawful under the Fourth Amendment
    E. Suppressed because Oscar was not advised of his rights

6. Officer Jones suspects Jimmy of murder. Without a search warrant, Officer Jones searches Jimmy's house, where he finds a diary that details the murder. At trial, if introduced into evidence against Jimmy, the diary most likely will be:
   A. Admitted because murder is a serious crime
   B. Admitted because Jimmy did not object to the search when it occurred
   C. Admitted because the diary is evidence of a crime
   D. Suppressed because the diary contains Jimmy's personal private thoughts
   E. Suppressed because the diary was obtained by an illegal search

7. In question # 6 above, the diary tells where Jimmy dumped the body. Police go to the location described in the diary and find the body lying in a ditch beside a highway. If offered into evidence at trial, the body most likely would be:
   A. Admitted because murder is a serious crime
   B. Admitted because the body would have been discovered eventually anyway
   C. Suppressed because it was found in an illegal search
   D. Suppressed because it derived from evidence obtained in an illegal search
   E. Suppressed unless an eyewitness can be found who saw Jimmy dump the body

8. Assistant high school Principal Romano learns that Todd is dealing drugs. She searches Todd's locker and finds a bag of marijuana. Romano turns the bag over to the police, who charge Todd with its illegal possession. If offered at trial as evidence, the marijuana will most likely be:
   A. Admitted because possession of marijuana is a crime
   B. Admitted because Romano was not acting at the direction of the police
   C. Admitted because the Fourth Amendment does not apply to children
   D. Suppressed because Romano did not have a search warrant
   E. Suppressed because Romano did not have Todd's permission to search his locker

9. Assistant Principal Romano thinks Jack may have marijuana in his locker. Romano calls the police and asks what to do. Police suggest that she search the locker. She does and finds the marijuana. If offered at trial, the marijuana will most likely be:
   A. Admitted because possession of marijuana is illegal
   B. Admitted because the search was offered at school
   C. Admitted because Romano is not a police officer
   D. Suppressed because Romano did not have a search warrant
   E. Suppressed because Romano was acting as an agent of the police

10. The case that established that evidence that is derived from illegally seized evidence is also not admissible in a criminal prosecution was:
   A. Wong Sun v. United States
   B. Williams v. Nix
   C. Michigan v. Long
   D. Hudson v. Palmer
   E. Gideon v. Wainwright

11. Officer Smith knowingly includes false statements in his application for a search warrant. Judge Schott reads the affidavit and issues the search warrant. Later at trial, the defendant objects to the evidence seized under the warrant. Under the "good faith" exception, the evidence most likely will be:
   A. Admitted because police obtained a search warrant
   B. Admitted if the judge who issued the warrant signed the warrant
   C. Admitted under the good faith exception established by Leon v. United States
   D. Suppressed because the affidavit in support of the search warrant was not submitted in good faith
   E. Suppressed, but only if Judge Schott knew that the statements in the affidavit were false

12. The police obtain a valid search warrant for cocaine in Oscar's house. Before officers arrive with the search warrant, other officers illegally enter Oscar's house and find the cocaine. If offered as evidence at trial, the cocaine will most likely be:
   A. Admitted because the possession of cocaine is illegal
   B. Admitted if police can show that they had an independent source for the information about the drugs being in the house other than the illegal entry
   C. Suppressed as the product of an illegal search
   D. Suppressed as evidence derived from evidence seized in an illegal search
   E. Suppressed unless Oscar gave consent for the search

13. Oscar is a passenger in Stan's car. Without probable cause or a search warrant, police stop and search Stan's car and find heroin under the passenger seat of the car. If introduced at trial against Oscar, the heroin will most likely be:
   A. Admitted because it illegal to possess heroin
   B. Admitted because Oscar does not have standing to object to an illegal search of Stan's car
   C. Suppressed because the search was without a search warrant
   D. Suppressed because the police did not have probable cause
   E. Suppressed because the drugs were found in Stan's car

14. Without a warrant, police illegally tap Malcolm's telephone and record conversations that show he is a principle in a drug conspiracy. If offered in evidence at trial, these recordings will be:
   A. Admissible because conspiracy to deal drugs is a crime
   B. Admissible because police did not trespass on Malcolm's property to overhear his conversations
   C. Suppressed because police invaded Malcolm's expectation of privacy
   D. Suppressed because police recorded his conversations, rather than just listening to them
   E. Suppressed, but only as Malcolm's conversations; those of the other party to the telephone call can be used in evidence

15. In order to obtain a search warrant, police must have evidence that the property to be seized is in the place where they want to search. The amount of evidence required to obtain a search warrant is:
    A. Suspicion
    B. Probable cause
    C. Proof beyond a reasonable doubt
    D. Clear and convincing evidence
    E. Absolute proof

16. The United States Supreme Court decision that changed the focus of Fourth Amendment violations from trespass into places to an intrusion on the expectation of privacy was:
    A. Mapp v. Ohio
    B. Gideon v. Wainwright
    C. Katz v. United States
    D. Wong Sun v. United States
    E. Weeks v. United States

17. The United States Supreme Court case that established the exclusionary rule and applied it against federal law enforcement officers was:
    A. Mapp v. Ohio
    B. Gideon v. Wainwright
    C. Katz v. United States
    D. Wong Sun v. United States
    E. Weeks v. United States

18. The United States Supreme Court case that established that information from anonymous informants could form part of the basis for probable cause to obtain a search warrant was:
    A. Mapp v. Ohio
    B. Gideon v. Wainwright
    C. Illinois v Gates
    D. Weeks v. United States
    E. Osgood v. Oregon

19. If the police illegality and the receipt of the evidence are separated in time, the exception to the fruit of the poisonous tree doctrine that may be used to get the evidence admitted at trial would be:
    A. Good faith
    B. Attenuation
    C. Independent source
    D. Inevitable discovery
    E. No expectation of privacy

20. The practice of state courts affording the accused greater protections under state law than that required by the United States Constitution is associated with the concept of:
    A. Due process
    B. The new freedom
    C. The new federalism
    D. Natural law doctrine
    E. Fruit of the poisonous tree doctrine

Essay Questions:

1. The primary purpose of the exclusionary rule is to discourage police misconduct. Does the rule achieve that purpose?

2. Police officers are advised in training to obtain a search warrant whenever possible because of Leon v. United States. Why is this true?

3. Does the requirement that the defendant have standing to object to an illegal search make sense in terms of the purposes of the exclusionary rule?

4. Before Mapp v. Ohio was decided, federal investigators who illegally seized evidence would turn the evidence over to state law enforcements officers for use at trial against the defendant in state court. Why?

5. Define probable cause in the context of obtaining a search warrant.

CHAPTER 4
ARREST

KEY TERMS AND CONCEPTS

AFFIDAVIT – A sworn statement in writing.

ARREST – The taking of a person into custody to bring them before a court to answer to a criminal charge.

ARREST WARRANT – A legal document that authorizes the arrest of the person named in the warrant.

BOOKING – a police administrative procedure officially recording an arrest in a police register.

COMMON LAW – A body of unwritten law developed in England and based on court decisions.

COMPLAINT – A written statement made under oath that sets forth the reasons why the person signing it believes that the person named in the complaint has committed a crime.

EXIGENT CIRCUMSTANCES – An emergency; any conditions and events that require immediate response.

EXTRADITION – a procedure whereby authorities in one state (the demanding state) demand from another state (the asylum state) that a fugitive from justice in the demanding state, who is present in the asylum state, be delivered to the demanding state.

FELONY – In most jurisdictions, a felony is defined as any crime that is or may be punished by death or imprisonment in a state prison.

FRESH PURSUIT - An officer's immediate pursuit of a criminal suspect into another jurisdiction after the officer has attempted to arrest the suspect in the officer's jurisdiction.

FRISK – A limited search for weapons.

HOT PURSUIT – The chasing of a fleeing felon by an officer.

MAGISTRATE – the judicial officer authorized to issue arrest warrants.

MISDEMEANOR – A crime for which the maximum possible sentence is less than one year's imprisonment.

PROBABLE CAUSE – In the context of an arrest, knowledge of facts and circumstances that would lead a reasonable person to believe that a crime has been committed and that it is more likely than not that the defendant did it. The amount of proof necessary to make a lawful arrest.

STOP –A brief seizure of a person for investigation based on an officer's reasonable suspicion of criminal activity, does not involve an intention to arrest.

SUMMONS – A document issued in the place of a custodial arrest that directs a person to appear in court at a time and place indicated to answer to a criminal charge.

KEY CASES

California v. Hodari D. (1990)

Ker v. Illinois (1886)

Tennessee v. Garner (1985)

Payton v. New York (1980)

Welsh v. Wisconsin (1984

CHAPTER OUTLINE

I. The power of arrest and its limitations
II. Definition of arrest
    A. Intention
    B. Real or pretend authority
    C. Detention or restraint
        i. Physical force
        ii. Show of authority
    D. Understanding by the person arrested
III. *De facto* arrest
    A. A seizure of the person tantamount to an arrest
IV. Arrest authority under a warrant
    A. Arrest warrant
    B. Complaint
    C. Probable cause
    D. Requirements for an arrest
    E. Summons
V. Arrest authority without a warrant
    A. Misdemeanor
        1. Probable cause
        2. Promptness
    B. Felony

1. Probable cause
2. Promptness

VI. Effecting a formal arrest
- A. Notice
- B. Time of day
- C. Service of summons
- D. Assistance
- E. Discretion

VII. Place of Arrest
- A. Fresh pursuit
- B. Citizen's authority to arrest

VIII. Use of Force
- A. Felony arrests
- B. Misdemeanor arrests
- C. Self-defense
- D. Resisting arrest

IX. Entry of dwellings
- A. Entry of the suspect's house
- B. Entry to the house of a third party
- C. Exigent circumstances
- D. Forced entry

X. Disposition on a person arrested
- A. Booking
- B. Initial appearance before the magistrate
- C. Safety considerations
- D. Protection and welfare of the arrested person
- E. Station house search
- F. Identification and examination of an arrested person

XI. The effect of an illegal arrest

REVIEW QUESTIONS

Fill in the blank:

1. Arrest is controlled by the _______________ Amendment to the United States Constitution.

2. The taking of a person into custody to appear before a court to answer a criminal charge is a(n) ____________________________.

3. A legal document that commands that a person named in the document be taken into custody is a(n) __________________________.

4. An arrest requires physical force or, where force is absent, ____________________ to the assertion of authority.

5. A touching, however slight, of the ________________of the accused is sufficient to effect an arrest.

6. An arrest can be made without touching if there is a show of ___________________ and the person to be arrested submits to arrest.

7. In order to make an arrest, the police officer must manifest a(n) _________________ to make an arrest.

8. An investigative stop is a brief _____________________ of a person for the purpose of determining whether a crime has been, is being, or is about to be committed.

9. The amount of evidence necessary to make a valid arrest is ____________________.

10. A seizure of a person that is tantamount to an arrest is called a _____________ arrest.

11. A law enforcement officer who has knowledge of an arrest warrant may make the arrest even though they do not have __________________ of the arrest warrant.

12. An application for an arrest warrant is called a(n) ____________________.

13. A _____________________ is a document that directs a person to appear before a court at a set time and place to answer to a criminal charge.

14. In most jurisdictions, a police officer without an arrest warrant can arrest for a _______________ if the offense is committed in their presence.

15. Warrantless arrests can be made in a public place if the police officer has ____________________ to believe that a felony has been committed, even though it was not committed in their presence.

16. A _________________ is a criminal offense, the punishment for which is more than one year in jail.

17. In most states, an officer without an arrest warrant can arrest a suspect in a case of fresh ___________________.

18. The decision of the United States Supreme Court that established when a police officer may use deadly force to stop a fleeing felon is ___________________.

19. The decision of the United States Supreme Court that held that police officers without an arrest warrant cannot enter a suspect's home to arrest him for a routine felony is ___________________________.

20. The United States Supreme Court decision that held that an illegal arrest did not prohibit the prosecution of a criminal defendant is ________________________.

True or False:

1. _____It is permissible to invite the news media to accompany you when serving an arrest warrant in a person's residence.

2. _____Misdemeanor arrests should be made without unreasonable delay.

3. _____Most jurisdictions require a police officer to have an arrest warrant to arrest a person for a misdemeanor not committed in the officer's presence.

4. _____A felony is a serious crime, the penalty for which the sentence is less than one year in jail.

5. _____Police can use as much force as they want to in making an arrest for a felony.

6. _____A person cannot be arrested by a police officer unless the police officer has an arrest warrant.

7. _____A complaint serves as the basis for the issuance of an arrest warrant.

8. _____The amount of probable cause to arrest without a warrant is the same amount of probable cause that you would need to get an arrest warrant.

9. _____Police in most jurisdictions can request citizens to assist them in effecting an arrest.

10. _____In most states, a police officer cannot arrest without a warrant outside his jurisdiction.

11. _____In most states, a police officer can arrest outside their jurisdiction in cases of fresh pursuit.

12. _____Generally, a police officer may use that amount of non-deadly force that is reasonable and necessary to overcome resistance when making an arrest.

13. _____Police can shoot a suspect who is a fleeing felon to keep them from getting away.

14. _____The United States Supreme Court limited the authority of police officers to use deadly force in the decision of Garner v. Tennessee.

15. _____In most jurisdictions, merely running away will not constitute resisting arrest.

16. _____A police officer would be justified in using deadly force if they reasonably believed they were about to suffer death or great bodily harm from an attacker.

17. _____A police officer is never justified in using deadly force to effect an arrest for a misdemeanor.

18. _____Under Payton v. New York, absent exigent circumstances, a police officer may not enter a suspect's residence without a warrant to make a felony arrest.

19. _____To arrest a suspect in the home of a third party, both an arrest warrant and a search warrant would be required.

20. _____Exigent circumstances may permit the warrantless entry into a suspect's home to effect an arrest.

Multiple Choice:

1. To make a lawful arrest, a police officer must always have:
   A. An arrest warrant
   B. Probable cause
   C. Two witnesses to the crime
   D. Handcuffs
   E. Permission from a judge

2. The United States Supreme Court case that established that an illegal arrest is not a bar to prosecution is:
   A. California v. Hodari D.
   B. Ker v. Illinois
   C. Payton v. New York
   D. Mapp v. Ohio
   E. Michigan v. Summers

3. Every arrest must be based upon evidence that would constitute:
   A. Suspicion
   B. Probable cause
   C. Proof beyond a reasonable doubt
   D. Clear and convincing evidence
   E. Absolute proof of guilt

4. Officer Smith observes Malcolm throw a brick through a jewelry store window. Officer Smith should:
   A. Arrest Malcolm and take him to the police station
   B. Go to the police station and obtain an arrest warrant for Malcolm's arrest
   C. Order Malcolm to remain at the jewelry store while he goes to get an arrest warrant
   D. Detain Malcolm until other officers can bring an arrest warrant to the scene of the crime
   E. Arrest Malcolm without a warrant, but only if the crime charged is a felony

5. Officer Jones develops information that, taken as a whole, leads him to believe that Roger has committed a burglary. Officer Jones should:
   A. Immediately locate Roger and arrest him without an arrest warrant
   B. Obtain an arrest warrant and go arrest Roger
   C. Wait until he has overwhelming evidence of Roger's guilt and then arrest him
   D. Interview Roger and, if he confesses to the burglary, arrest him
   E. Arrest Roger, interrogate him and, if he confesses, use his confession to obtain an arrest warrant

6. Officer Williams has probable cause to believe that Todd has committed arson, a felony. Officer Williams learns that Todd is hiding in Sue's house. In order to legally arrest Todd, Officer Williams will need:
   A. An arrest warrant
   B. An arrest warrant and a search warrant
   C. A large fire ax to break down Sue's door
   D. Handcuffs

7. Officer Wilson is in hot pursuit of Oscar, who has robbed a bank. Oscar abandons his car and runs into his house and hides under his bed. Under the law, Officer Wilson:
   A. Can enter Oscar's house without a warrant and arrest him
   B. Must go and get a warrant for Oscar's arrest
   C. Can enter Oscar's house, but only if he has Oscar's consent
   D. Must have the victim of the crime with him when he enters Oscar's house
   E. Must call a judge and get permission to enter Oscar's house without a warrant

8. Officer Able is chasing a shoplifter who stole a radio from a retail store. The shoplifter jumps into a garbage dumpster to hide from the police. In order for Officer Able to arrest the shoplifter:
   A. He must have an arrest warrant
   B. He must have a search warrant
   C. He must have either an arrest warrant or a search warrant
   D. He needs neither an arrest warrant or a search warrant to remove the shoplifter from the dumpster
   E. He needs permission from the company that owns the dumpster to remove the shoplifter

9. Officer Thomas arrests a subject for a misdemeanor theft. Before she can get the subject handcuffed, he breaks away from her and runs down the street. With regard to using deadly force:
   A. Officer Thomas may use deadly force to prevent the subject's escape
   B. Officer Thomas may use deadly force to prevent the escape, but only after ordering the subject to halt
   C. Officer Thomas may use deadly force to prevent the escape of the subject, but only after yelling for him to halt and firing a warning shot
   D. Officer Thomas is not permitted to use deadly force to stop a person who has committed a misdemeanor

10. The United States Supreme Court case that established guidelines for the use of deadly force in stopping a fleeing felon was:
    A. Garner v. Tennessee
    B. Mapp v. Ohio
    C. Payton v. New York
    D. Ker v. Illinois
    E. Gideon v. Wainwright

11. Officer Bello has probable cause to believe that Mike is dealing cocaine, a felony. Officer Bello goes over the Mike's house, but does not have an arrest warrant or a search warrant. As Officer Bello approaches the house, Mike, who is standing in the front yard, suddenly runs into the house and yells to his girlfriend, "Quick, Helen, flush the crack down the toilet. It's the cops!" As Officer Bello approaches the front door, he hears the toilet flush. On these facts, Officer Bello can:
    A. Enter the house without a search warrant, and arrest Mike
    B. Leave the house and find a judge who will issue a search warrant
    C. Enter the house, but only if Mike gives his permission
    D. Stay at the house and arrest Mike if he comes out of the house
    E. Enter the house and seize the drugs, but not arrest Mike because he lacks an arrest warrant

12. Officer Dane arrests Susan on a warrant charging her with prostitution. At the police station during the booking process, Officer Dane searches Susan's purse and finds cocaine. If offered into evidence at trial, the cocaine will be:
    A. Admitted because possession of cocaine is a crime
    B. Admitted because it was found during the booking process after a lawful arrest
    C. Suppressed because Officer Dane lacked probable cause to look in the purse
    D. Suppressed unless Officer Dane has a search warrant for the purse
    E. Suppressed unless Officer Dane had Susan's permission to look in her purse

13. Officer Smith receives a radio call of an armed robbery at a drug store. Upon Officer Smith's arrival at the scene, a taxi driver reports that he followed the suspect from the drug store to a residence a block away. Officer Smith goes to the residence and knocks at the door. An elderly woman answers the door. Officer Smith asks her if anyone else was in the house, and she says "no." Officers immediately remove the female from the house to a place of safety and enter the house. In a bedroom, they find the suspect pretending to be asleep, and in the basement they find the gun that was used and the money that was taken. Concerning this matter, it can be said that:
    A. This was a lawful search and arrest due to exigent circumstances
    B. This was a lawful search, but the arrest was illegal because police lacked an arrest warrant
    C. Both the search and the arrest were unlawful because police lacked both an arrest warrant and a search warrant
    D. This was a lawful arrest, but the search was illegal because police did not have a search warrant

14. Farmer Brown sees Kazmaier trespassing on his land. Trespass is a misdemeanor. Brown calls Sheriff Westrick. When Westrick gets to the farm, Brown tells him that he wants Kazmaier arrested. In most states, Sheriff Westrick should:
    A. Advise Brown that there is nothing that he can do since he did not see Kazmier commit the crime
    B. Arrest Kazmier for trespass
    C. Advise Brown that, if he wants Kazmier arrested, he will have to do it himself
    D. Have Brown go to the station and sign a complaint so that an arrest warrant may be issued

15. After a person is arrested, the police will take them into to the police station for a procedure called:
    A. Information
    B. Consent
    C. Search
    D. Indictment
    E. Booking

16. Generally, a person who is arrested must be brought before a judge for an initial appearance within:
    A. One hour
    B. Two hours
    C. Forty-eight hours
    D. Five days
    E. Thirty days

17. Roger kills a police officer and flees to Canada. Without waiting for an arrest warrant or formal extradition proceedings, police officers drive to Canada, locate Roger, handcuff him, throw him into the car, and drive him back to the United States. At trial, Roger argues that the charges against him should be thrown out because he was arrested illegally. The Judge should:
    A. Throw out the charges and release Roger
    B. Throw out the charges and release Roger, but allow police to re-arrest him
    C. Throw out the charges, release Roger to the custody of the officers, and let them handle the matter as they see fit
    D. Allow the trial to proceed, using all evidence lawfully obtained against Roger
    E. Allow the trial to proceed, but penalize the prosecution for the illegal arrest by limiting the number of witnesses that they can call

18. Officer Robbins responds to a complaint of a disorderly patron at a bar. Upon arrival, the manager points out George, who is noisily celebrating. Officer Robbins approaches George and tells him to quiet down or leave. George slaps Officer Robbins in the face. Before Officer Robbins can react, George, realizing what he has done, surrenders to Officer Robbins and submits to arrest. On the facts, Officer Robbins should:

A. Take George into custody and transport him to the station
B. Punch George once in the head to make it even and then arrest George
C. Take George outside, use his baton to adjust George's attitude, and then arrest George
D. Take George out of the bar and drop him off in a remote area out of town without any clothes
E. Spray George with pepper spray, strike him with a baton and punch him in the nose, and write the report that George was still resisting arrest when he did so

19. Officer Wayne arrests Chad without an arrest warrant and without probable cause. At the station, police search Chad and find marijuana. Concerning this arrest, it can be said that:

A. Because the arrest is illegal, the search is illegal and the marijuana will be suppressed
B. The arrest is illegal, but the drugs will be admissible at trial
C. The drugs can be used as probable cause for the arrest
D. Officer Wayne should change his report to show that the marijuana was found before the arrest was made
E. Because the arrest was illegal, Officer Wayne should give Chad back his marijuana

20. The United States Supreme Court decision that requires police officers to have an arrest warrant before entering a suspect's house to arrest them is:

A. Ker v. Illinois
B. Payton v. New York
C. Belton v. New York
D. Baker v. Carr
E. Terry v. Ohio

Essay Questions:

1. When would police use a summons instead of making a physical arrest?

2. If Ker v. Illinois ... od law (and it is!), why should police worry about the formalities of searc... eizure and arrest and not just go get the suspect?

3. If a police officer can arrest without an arrest warrant for a felony, why do we encourage them to get the arrest warrant before taking the person into custody?

4. How much force can a police officer use when effecting an arrest?

5. The law in most jurisdictions prohibits a person from resisting an arrest, even if the person knows the arrest is unlawful. Why?

8. ________________ is anything that tends to prove or disprove an issue in question.

9. Criminal tools could be seized with a search warrant because they are ____________________.

10. The Fourth Amendment requires that the place to be searched be described with ____________________, as well as the items or persons to be seized.

11. A written statement made under oath that the statement is true is called an ____________________.

12. Police may ____________________ a residence to keep people out while they obtain a search warrant.

13. A search warrant issued to allow a search of a place where contraband will be at a future time is called a(n) ____________________ search warrant.

14. Generally, when searching a residence with a search warrant, police officers must knock and __________________ their presence before entering.

15. A scope of the search warrant is the _________________ that can be searching within the building under that warrant.

16. School officials may search ____________________without a warrant in order to maintain safety and security within the school.

17. Electronic surveillance requires that officers have obtained a valid ____________________.

18. Under the exclusionary rule, illegally seized evidence is ____________________in a criminal trial against the defendant.

19. Title III of the Omnibus Crime Control and Safe Streets Act of 1968 requires ____________________supervision of electronic surveillance by the police.

20. A(n) __________________search is a search of a business to determine if they are in compliance with codes and licensing provisions dealing with fire, health, safety, etc.

True or False:

1. _____All searches by police require a search warrant.

2. _____The chief of police may issue a search warrant.

3. _____The judge issuing a search warrant must be neutral and detached from the case.

4. _____If police officers knowingly falsify their statements to obtain a search warrant, any evidence seized under that warrant will be inadmissible at trial.

5. _____Police have a valid search warrant for a house at 123 Elm Street. Upon arrival at that location, an informant tells them that the property they are looking for is now at 400 Main Street. Police can just cross out 123 Elm Street and write in 400 Main Street, and then go to that location and conduct a search.

6. _____A search warrant for "a white house on Main Street in Whoseville" would meet the specificity requirement of the Fourth Amendment.

7. _____A search warrant can be issued to allow the search of a person.

8. _____A description in a search warrant listing the items to be seized as "obscene materials" would be sufficient.

9. _____In a search warrant, a general description will not be permitted if a more specific description is possible.

10. _____A law enforcement officer may submit more than one affidavit in support of an application for a search warrant.

11. _____Police officers may secure a dwelling to prevent persons from entering until a search warrant can be obtained.

12. _____An anticipatory search warrant is one that is issued to search a particular place for a particular item that has not yet arrived at that place where the search warrant is to be executed.

13. _____A search warrant may be executed only by the officer or class of officers named in the warrant.

14. _____Some jurisdictions restrict nighttime search warrants.

15. _____When serving a search warrant, officers must generally knock and announce their presence before entering the premises.

16. _____Exigent circumstances, like the destruction of evidence, may merit police to enter without knocking and announcing their presence.

17. _____A search warrant for a place authorizes police to search everyone found at that place.

18. _____Police officers serving a search warrant may search only where the items described in the warrant may reasonably be concealed.

19. _____Officers executing a search warrant may use reasonable force to enter the premises.

20. _____A law enforcement officer serving a search warrant may seize items not listed in the warrant if they are found in plain view during the search and are immediately recognizable as contraband.

Multiple Choice:

1. Officer Jones has a valid search warrant to look for a stolen automobile at 123 Elm Street. At 123 Elm Street, Officer Smith may legally look in the:
   A. Bathroom
   B. Kitchen cabinets
   C. Hall closet
   D. Garage
   E. Attic

2. Officer Smith is serving a valid search warrant for marijuana in a house. Officer Smith may look for the marijuana:
   A. Only in the living room
   B. Only in the garage
   C. Only in the bathroom
   D. Only under the mattress in the bedroom
   E. Any area where marijuana could be concealed

3. Officer Wilson has a valid search warrant to search for cocaine in Oscar's apartment. While serving the search warrant, Officer Wilson observes what her training and experience has taught her to be heroin. Officer Wilson may:
   A. Not seize the heroin because the search warrant was for cocaine
   B. Not seize the heroin unless Oscar gives her permission to take it
   C. May seize the heroin, but cannot use it in evidence against Oscar
   D. May seize the heroin, but can only use it in evidence against Oscar if she finds cocaine, also
   E. May seize the heroin and charge Oscar with its illegal possession

4. A search warrant may be issued by:
   A. The governor
   B. The prosecutor
   C. The court bailiff
   D. A judge
   E. The sheriff of the county where the search is to take place

5. In order to obtain a search warrant, the amount of evidence that the officer needs is:
   A. Suspicion
   B. Probable cause
   C. Proof beyond a reasonable doubt
   D. Clear and convincing evidence
   E. Absolute proof

6. Oscar, a confidential police informant, tells Officer Robbins that three months ago he bought heroin from John in John's basement in the residence at 123 Elm Street. Officer Robbins prepares an affidavit setting forth these facts and takes it to a judge to obtain a search warrant. It is most likely that:
   A. The judge will issue the warrant based on probable cause
   B. The judge will issue the warrant, but only for the basement, not the whole house
   C. The judge will not issue the warrant because Officer Robbins did not see the heroin
   D. The judge will not issue the warrant because Oscar does not have a sample of the heroin he obtained
   E. The judge will not issue the warrant because the probable cause is stale

7. A credit card used to steal money from an automatic teller machine could be seized under a search warrant as:
   A. Fruits of the crime
   B. Instrumentalities
   C. Evidence
   D. Contraband

8. Officer Martin gets an anonymous telephone call indicating that Oscar is dealing drugs out of his apartment. Concerning this anonymous tip, it can be said that:
   A. Standing alone it is probable cause to obtain a search warrant
   B. Standing alone it is not enough to get a search warrant
   C. It can never be used as part of the probable cause to obtain a search warrant
   D. It is not enough for a search warrant, but would justify a warrantless search of Oscar's apartment
   E. Should be ignored by Officer Martin, as it is most likely a prank call

9. Interpretations of the Fourth Amendment to the United States Constitution protect:
   A. Homes

10. Concerning a search warrant, it can be said that:
   A. Police officers may issue them if they have the rank of captain or above
   B. Some jurisdictions allow police to request a search warrant by telephone
   C. Once issued, a search warrant is good forever and can be used anytime
   D. Can be issued "in blank" so that police can fill in the location later when it is determined
   E. Must be served by civilians whenever possible

Essay Questions:

1. What are the advantages of a telephonic search warrant?

2. What is the scope of a search warrant issued for a stolen washing machine at 123 Elm Street?

3. Why should search warrants be issued by judges rather than by prosecutors?

4. Under what circumstances would officers be permitted to ignore the "knock and announce" requirement when serving a search warrant?

5. Under what circumstances may police detain persons found at a location where a search warrant is being served? Can these detained persons be searched?

10. During a stop, police may use reasonable _________________ to prevent the suspect from walking away.

11. On a traffic stop, officers may develop information sufficient to justify not only a frisk of the driver, but also of the ______________________.

12. In Illinois v. Wardlow, running from the police was held to be sufficient to justify a ________________________ of the person.

13. A series of individually lawful acts may provide reasonable suspicion of criminal activity sufficient to justify a ______________________.

14. Roadblocks that constitute roadside safety checks have been held to be ____________________.

15. Stopping vehicles solely based on the race of the driver is called ______________________.

16. Stopping a person solely because they were in a high crime area would be ______________________.

17. A suitcase could be detained for a canine examination if the suitcase was held for only a _______________________ period of time.

18. Miranda warnings are ___________________ when making a Terry stop.

19. The reason that the Courts have permitted police to order the driver and passengers out of a vehicle on a traffic stop is a concern for the officer's __________________.

20. What is reasonable in a given situation will be determined by a _________________.

True or false:

1. _____Every stop always justifies a frisk.

2. _____A stop requires probable cause to believe that a crime has been committed.

3. _____A stop can be justified on reasonable suspicion that a crime is going to be committed.

4. _____The purpose of a stop is investigation.

5. _____A stop c[illegible] only be for a reasonable amount of time.

6. ____ [illegible]g a stop, the suspect is free to go.

7. _____During a stop, the suspect is under arrest.

8. _____The investigation during a stop may reveal information that will justify an arrest.

9. _____A person who is stopped must be given Miranda warnings.

10. _____A lawful stop requires that the officer have reasonable suspicion.

11. _____Flight from a police officer can justify a stop.

12. _____While a stop requires suspicion, police can have a contact with a person without any particularized suspicion at all.

13. _____Police can walk up to a person and ask them to empty their pockets.

14. _____Police can stop a person they suspect has committed a crime.

15. _____Suspicion and probable cause are the same thing.

16. _____Information from informants can be the basis for a stop.

17. _____An anonymous tip that a suspect is standing on a sidewalk alone would be sufficient evidence to stop and frisk.

18. _____Police may rely on a radio broadcast for information to justify a stop.

19. _____A police officer who makes a traffic stop may order the driver out of the car.

20. _____A police officer who makes a traffic stop may order the driver and passengers to stay in the car.

Multiple choice:

1. The United States Supreme Court decision that permits officers to stop and frisk suspects is:
    - A. Illinois v. Gates
    - B. Terry v. Ohio
    - C. Mapp v. Ohio
    - D. Ker v. California
    - E. Sibron v. New York

2. A police officer who makes a lawful traffic stop can:
   A. Order the driver out of the car
   B. Order the passengers out of the car
   C. Order the driver to stay in the car
   D. Order the passengers to stay in the car
   E. All of the above are permissible

3. A frisk is a pat down of the outer garments looking for:
   A. Drugs
   B. Evidence of a crime
   C. Weapons
   D. Drug paraphernalia

4. Officer Jones observes a car with two male occupants parked in an area that is considered a high crime area with heavy drug activity. Which of the following facts would contribute to justification for a stop?
   A. Other subjects approach the car on foot, talk briefly with the passenger of the car and then leave
   B. The driver of the car is known to the officer to be a drug dealer
   C. The car pulls away quickly as the police approach
   D. As police approach the car, the passenger leans forward and puts something under the front seat of the car
   E. All of the above are facts that support a stop of the vehicle

5. Concerning a stop, it can be said that:
   A, The purpose of the stop is to investigate criminal activity
   B. The stop must be based on probable cause
   C. Police may detain the person for as long as they want to
   D. During a stop, the person detained is free to go

6. Concerning a stop, it is important to remember that:
   A. No force can be used to detain the person
   B. Any person stopped may also be frisked
   C. Information learned during the stop can not be used to justify an arrest
   D. The person stopped is in custody the same as if he were under arrest
   E. The duration of the stop must be reasonable given the circumstances of the stop

7. During a stop and frisk, it would be lawful for the police officer to:
   A. Reach into the suspect's pocket and remove whatever they found
   B. Search a book bag that the suspect was carrying
   C. Ask the suspect if they had a weapon on their person
   D. Require the suspect to remove all their clothing

8. During a stop and frisk, it should be remembered that:
   A. Miranda warnings must be give before asking any questions
   B. The stop and frisk can only be done in a public area like a sidewalk
   C. The suspect is under arrest and should be handcuffed
   D. Both the stop and the frisk need to be independently justified

9. Concerning a stop and frisk, it should be remembered that:
   A. The frisk must always come before the stop
   B. Only male officers can frisk male suspects
   C. Only female officers should stop and frisk female suspects
   D. The stop should be based only on a racial profile
   E. The frisk is a pat down of the external garments looking for weapons

10. The purpose of the frisk is to:
   A. Harass the suspect
   B. Look for illegal drugs
   C. Find evidence of a crime
   D. Promote officer safety
   E. Exercise police authority

11. Which United States Supreme Court decision held that an anonymous tip that a suspect had a gun and was standing alone was insufficient justification for a stop and frisk?
   A. Terry v. Ohio
   B. Illinois v. Wardlow
   C. Florida v. J.L.
   D. Maryland v. Wilson
   E. Gideon v. Wainwright

12. Which United States Supreme Court decision held that the act of running from the police alone gave officers sufficient justification for a stop?
   A. Terry v. Ohio
   B. Illinois v. Wardlow
   C. Florida v. J.L.
   D. Maryland v. Wilson
   E. Gideon v. Wainwright

Essay Questions:

1. What amount of proof of criminal wrongdoing is needed to justify a stop?

2. What is the scope of a frisk?

3. An officer observes a subject walking down the sidewalk in a residential area of town at 10:00 a.m. on a Tuesday. The officer has never seen the subject before and does not recognize him as a resident of the area. What actions, if any, would the officer be justified in taking based on these facts? Why?

4. An officer on patrol at 3:00 a.m. observes a car pull out from behind a retail store that has been closed since 9:00 p.m. The car does not have its headlights on, but the driver turns them on before entering the street. There are two male subjects in the car. What actions, if any would the officer be justified in taking on these facts? Why?

5. While on patrol, you receive a radio call that there has been an armed robbery of a convenience store one mile from your location. The robbery occurred ten minutes ago, and the radio broadcast describes the robber as a white male, 25 years old, with blond hair, and wearing a blue windbreaker, a Chicago cubs baseball hat, and blue jeans. Taken in the offense was a white paper bag containing an unknown amount of currency. At that moment, you observe a white male about 21 years old with blond hair walking down the sidewalk carrying a white paper bag. The subject you see has blue jeans, but no jacket or hat. What action would you be justified in taking on these facts? Why?

11. If police arrest a person, they can search any __________________ that the person is carrying, like a briefcase or book bag.

12. Police may arrest a person for one crime and, during the search incident to a lawful arrest, find evidence that the person has committed another different __________________.

13. A container is any object capable of holding another _____________________.

14. When making an arrest in a residence, police may make a protective _____________________ of the residence to make certain that the premises are safe.

15. During the protective sweep, officers may observe evidence in ________________ and can seize it.

16. In order for a search incident to a lawful arrest to be legal, the arrest itself must be based on __________________________.

True or False:

1. _____A search incident to a lawful arrest must be based upon probable cause.

2. _____For the search incident to a lawful arrest to be legal, the arrest must be custodial.

3. _____Searches incident to a lawful arrest require a search warrant.

4. _____Under Belton v. New York, the custodial arrest of a passenger in an automobile justifies the search of the entire passenger compartment of the car and any containers in the passenger compartment.

5. _____For a search incident to an arrest to be lawful, the arrest must be lawful.

6. _____If a person was arrested while sitting at a desk, police could lawfully search the drawers of the desk.

7. _____If a person arrested asks to get their coat out of the closet, the police will be able to search the closet.

8. _____A container is any object capable of holding another object.

9. _____There are no limits on where police can search incident to a lawful arrest.

10. _____Under a search incident to a lawful arrest, police could search the passenger compartment of an automobile that had been driven by the subject arrested, even though the subject had been removed from the car and was sitting in a police car in handcuffs.

11. ______A companion of the person arrested may be searched if the officer suspects the companion has a weapon or may destroy evidence.

12. ______A protective sweep of the premises where a person is arrested is justified if the officers have a reasonable concern that other suspects may be hiding on the premises.

13. ______The purpose of a protective sweep is to look for evidence.

14. ______After a lawful arrest, police may delay making the search incident to it for as long as they like.

15. ______A search incident to a lawful arrest may actually occur before the arrest is made.

16. ______Police may use reasonable force to conduct a search incident to a lawful custodial arrest.

17. ______Police may arrest a person who is detained if they have probable cause to arrest and if there is the likelihood that evidence will be destroyed.

18. ______A search incident to a lawful arrest is unlimited in scope.

19. ______Only evidence of the crime for which a defendant was arrested can be used against the defendant after a search incident to a lawful arrest.

20. ______If a police officer stops a driver to issue a speeding ticket, the officer may search the car under the exception known as "search incident to arrest."

Multiple Choice:

1. The United States Supreme Court decision that allows the search of an automobile from which a passenger has just been arrested is:
   - A. Buie v. Maryland
   - B. Belton v. New York
   - C. Chimel v. California
   - D. Terry v. Ohio
   - E. Scott v. Illinois

2. The purpose of a protective sweep is to:
   - A. Protect officers making the arrest
   - B. Check the house for hazardous materials
   - C. Find evidence of the crime for which the suspect was arrested
   - D. Find evidence of crimes other than the one for which the person was arrested

3. The justification for a search incident to a lawful arrest is to prevent the destruction of evidence and to look for:
   A. Evidence of other crimes
   B. Weapons
   C. Contraband
   D. Stolen property

4. In a search incident to a lawful arrest, police could not search a suspect's:
   A. Pants pockets
   B. Wallet
   C. Hat
   D. Jacket pockets
   E. Locked desk drawer

5. Police enter a residence to arrest Oscar with a valid arrest warrant. Oscar is sitting on the couch in the living room eating popcorn. Incident to a lawful arrest, police may search all of the following **except:**
   A. Oscar's pants pockets
   B. Under the couch
   C. In the couch under the cushions
   D. The coat closet in the hallway
   E. The popcorn bowl from which Oscar was eating

6. Police arrest Mary for shoplifting. Incidental to the arrest, police can search all of the following **except:**
   A. Mary's book bag she was wearing when arrested
   B. Mary's purse
   C. Mary's billfold that was inside the purse
   D. A package of cigarettes that Mary had in her purse
   E. Mary's car parked at her residence

7. Bill is a passenger in Todd's car. Police stop Todd for speeding and determine that there is an active arrest warrant for Bill. Police arrest Bill and place him in their patrol car. Police can now search:
   A. The entire passenger compartment of Todd's car and everything in it
   B. The passenger compartment of Todd's car, but not Todd's coat in the car
   C. The passenger compartment of Todd's car, but not Bill's book bag in the car
   D. Any property Bill had in the car, but nobody else's stuff
   E. Only those areas of the passenger compartment Bill could have reached from where he was sitting

8. Oscar is a passenger in Chad's car. Police stop Chad for speeding and determine that there is an active arrest warrant for Oscar for stealing a piano. Under the law governing search incident to a lawful arrest, police can search:
   A. Chad's car, but only where a piano could be concealed
   B. The trunk of Chad's car
   C. The passenger compartment of Chad's car
   D. Only that area of Chad's car where Oscar was sitting
   E. No part of the car, because Oscar was only a passenger in Chad's car

9. Oscar is a passenger in Larry's car. Police stop Larry for speeding and arrest him because there is a valid arrest warrant charging him with possession of cocaine. Under the law of search incident to lawful arrest, police can search:
   A. All of Larry's car, including the trunk
   B. The passenger compartment but only containers that belonged to Larry
   C. Larry's coat, but not Oscar's coat
   D. Oscar's coat, but not Larry's coat
   E. Both Oscar and Larry's coat if they were in the passenger compartment of the car

10. Officer Johnson stops Mary solely because of her race and arrests her without probable cause. Under the law governing searches incidental to arrest, it can be said that:
   A. Officer Jones can search Mary's person
   B. Officer Jones can search Mary's clothing
   C. Officer Jones can search any containers Mary was carrying when she was arrested
   D. Officer Jones can search Mary's car
   E. No search will be lawful because the arrest was unlawful

Essay Questions:

1.When can police search a companion of a person who is arrested?

2. What are the two purposes of a search incident to a lawful arrest?

3. What is the purpose of a protective sweep of the premises where a person is arrested?

4. Police meet Oscar's plane when it arrives at the airport and arrest him on a warrant charging him with possession of illegal weapons. Police take Oscar to the baggage claim area and pick up his suitcase when it comes off the conveyor belt. Can police search the suitcase without a warrant incident to Oscar's lawful arrest? Why?

5. Officer Malcolm arrests Todd for burglary pursuant to a valid arrest warrant. During the search incidental to the arrest, Officer Malcolm finds an ounce of cocaine in Todd's pants pocket. At his trial for burglary, the jury finds Todd not guilty. Can the cocaine that was found in Todd's pocket still be used to prosecute him for possession of cocaine?

3. Police can request consent to search even though they do not have __________________, which would be required to obtain a search warrant.

4. In obtaining consent, police cannot use force, coercion, or __________________.

5. In order to introduce evidence seized in a consent search, the prosecution must introduce "clear and convincing evidence" that the consent to search was given ______________________.

6. Courts will usually find that consent was involuntary if the police used threats or physical ______________________ to obtain the consent.

7. A suspect may be forcibly stopped and still give voluntary _________________ to search afterwards.

8. If an officer with a search warrant wants to obtain consent to search, they must obtain consent ____________________ showing the suspect the search warrant.

9. An undercover officer can conceal their identity as a police officer and still obtain a valid _______________________ to search.

10. A person who is under arrest can still voluntarily _________________ to a search.

11. If the arrest of the subject is illegal, any consent that was subsequently given was invalid, and evidence found as a result of that search will be ___________________.

12. An invitation to enter a building is not the same as a consent to _______________ the building.

13. An officer who is invited to enter may seize contraband that they see in _________________ within the room.

14. Courts have held that the scope of a consent search is limited by the concept of _________________________.

15. If a significant period of time has passed since a consent was given, before resuming the search the officers should obtain a new __________________.

16. Permission to search an automobile would include consent to search a ________________ in the car where the item sought might be concealed.

17. A husband and wife have equal authority to give consent to search to property that they own _____________________.

18. Whether a consent was voluntary or not will ultimately be decided by a ____________________.

19. A parent can consent to a search of property owned by the parent even if occupied by a minor ________________ living at home.

20. The key to a lawful consent search is that the consent was given _________________ by someone with authority to give consent.

True or False:

1. _____In order to be a valid search, consent to search must be given voluntarily.

2. _____Police may use promises, but not force or threats, to obtain consent to search.

3. _____Police must advise a subject that they have a right to refuse to give consent before asking for consent to search.

4. _____A person who is under arrest cannot voluntarily consent to a search.

5. _____A person's knowledge that they had a right to refuse to give consent to a search would indicate that the consent they did give was given voluntarily.

6. _____Threatening to arrest a subject if they did not consent to a search would make any consent they gave involuntary.

7. _____When the court determines that the consent was not given voluntarily, evidence seized during the search will be suppressed.

8. _____After a traffic stop, the officer must advise the motorist that they are free to go, before requesting consent to search the car.

9. _____Police must use a written consent to search form in order to obtain a valid consent to search.

10. _____A person's intelligence and education may be a factor in determining whether consent was voluntarily given.

11. _____The fact that a suspect does not speak fluent English may be a factor in determining whether their consent was voluntary.

12. _____Permission to search a car for a stolen guitar would give officers permission to search any containers in the car, no matter how small.

13. _____A person who gives consent to search may revoke that consent at any time.

14. _____A person giving consent to search may place limitations on the scope of that search.

15. _____The only person able to give consent is one whose constitutional protection against unreasonable searches and seizures would be violated by a search without consent.

16. _____A third party may consent to a search if they have common authority over the area to be searched.

17. _____If the tenant has signed a lease, the landlord may give consent to search the tenant's apartment.

18. _____A motel manager who owns the motel may give consent to search a guest's motel room.

19. _____An employer may consent to search an area set aside for the employee and where the employee has exclusive control.

20. _____A school principal can consent to a search of a student's locker.

Multiple Choice:

1. Oscar and Ted are roommates in an apartment. Each has their own bedroom, but they share the bathroom, kitchen and living room. The police arrive at the apartment and ask Ted for consent to search. Ted can consent to a search:
   A. Of the entire apartment
   B. Of the entire apartment, if he pays at least one half the monthly rent
   C. The kitchen, bathroom and living room
   D. The kitchen, bathroom, living room, and his bedroom, but not Oscar's bedroom

2. Mary is a guest at a party at Chad's house. The police knock on the door, and since Chad and the other guests are in the kitchen, Mary opens the door. The police ask for consent to come in and search the house. Mary can:
   A. Give the officers consent to enter and search the house
   B. Give the officers consent to enter, but not to search
   C. Give consent to search, but not to enter
   D. Not give permission to enter or search Chad's house

3. The police get a report of a loud party in a motel room. They go to the motel and ask the manager for consent to search the motel room. The manager gives his consent. The police:
   A. Can search the motel room
   B. Can search the motel room, but only if they had probable cause
   C. Cannot search the room based on the consent of the motel manager
   D. Can search, but only if the officers have reasonable suspicion that underaged drinking is occurring in the motel room

4. The police go to Oscar's house because they suspect he is dealing cocaine. They do not have a search warrant or an arrest warrant. The police knock on the door and tell Oscar that they will arrest him if he does not give them consent to search. Oscar consents to a search and the police find cocaine in the bedroom in a dresser drawer. Concerning the search, it is:
   A. Valid if Oscar owns the house
   B. Invalid because Oscar's wife did not give her consent to the search
   C. Invalid because the police did not have probable cause
   D. Invalid because the police used coercion to get Oscar to consent
   E. Invalid because the cocaine was not in plain view in the house

5. The police stop Terry and ask permission to search his car. Terry agrees, and the police find marijuana in the console of the car. This search will be lawful if:
   A. The police told Terry he was free to go before obtaining consent
   B. The police obtained a written consent to search
   C. The police did not have any suspicion that Terry possessed marijuana
   D. The police obtained from Terry's consent that was voluntary

6. The police want to search Mark's car. They approach Mark in a parking lot and threaten to smash the headlight of his car unless he consents to a search. The police then have Mark sign a consent to search form. With regards to this search, it can be said that it is:
   A. Valid because the police did not threaten Mark, only his car
   B. Valid because Mark signed a written consent to search form
   C. Valid if the police find contraband in his car
   D. Invalid because his consent was not voluntary

7. The police go to 123 Elm Street to search the house for heroin. They have probable cause but do not have a search warrant. The police knock on the front door and a young woman answers. They ask the woman for consent to search the house and she consents. The police then find heroin concealed in a flowerpot in the basement. Concerning this search, it can be said it is:
   A. Lawful if the woman was someone authorized to give consent to search
   B. Lawful, but only because the police had probable cause
   C. Unlawful because the police did not have a search warrant
   D. Unlawful because the police exceeded the reasonable scope of her consent
   E. Unlawful because the police did not have her sign a written consent to search form

8. The police have suspicion that Todd is selling marijuana at the high school. They go to the high school and ask the principal for consent to search Todd's locker. The police find marijuana in Todd's locker. This search is:
   A. Lawful because school authorities can consent to a search of a student's locker
   B. Lawful because possession of marijuana is a crime
   C. Unlawful because Todd did not give consent to the search
   D. Unlawful because the police only had suspicion and not probable cause

9. The police have probable cause to believe that there is stolen property in Chad's house at 123 Elm Street. They obtain a valid search warrant and go to Chad's house. The police knock on the door and, when Chad answers the door, show him the search warrant and ask Chad for consent to search his house. Chad gives consent. Concerning this search, it can be said that:
   A. The police should have asked Chad for consent before showing him the search warrant
   B. The police should have not gotten the search warrant but only relied on Chad's consent
   C. The police should not have asked consent, but relied solely on the search warrant
   D. The police should have asked Chad's consent before obtaining the search warrant
   E. The police should have advised Chad of his right to refuse to give consent before asking him for consent

10. Ralph is driving his car down Main Street, and Sam is a passenger in Ralph's car. Ralph stops for gasoline, and the police approach his car and ask permission to search the car for marijuana. Ralph gives consent and the police find marijuana in Sam's book bag. Concerning this search, it can be said that:
   A. The police need probable cause to search Ralph's car
   B. The police should have obtained Ralph and Sam's consent to search the car
   C. The police were authorized by Ralph's consent to look in any container in the car where marijuana could be concealed
   D. The police can search the car with Ralph's permission but need a search warrant to search any containers they find in the car
   E. The police need the consent of the owner of the gasoline station and Ralph before searching the car because the car is on the property of the gasoline station

11. Mary, Helen and Sue purchase a boat, with each paying one third of the cost. During the summer, the three use the boat on alternating weekends. One Saturday while Sue is using the boat, the police harbor patrol sees Sue at the marina and asks for consent to search the boat. They find cocaine in the cabin of the boat. Concerning this search, it can be said that:
   A. Sue has authority to grant consent to a search of the boat
   B. The police must obtain consent from all three owners to search the boat
   C. The police must obtain permission from a majority of the owners to search the boat
   D. The police can only search one third of the boat with Sue's permission
   E. The police can search, but only if they had probable cause to believe that there were drugs on the boat before they asked Sue for consent to search

12. The police go to Roger's house to seek consent to search his garage for a stolen bicycle. They knock on Roger's door and ask if they can search his garage. Roger says nothing but comes outside the house and goes over to the garage where he opens the door. The police find the stolen bicycle. Concerning this search, it can be said that:
    A. The search is unlawful because Roger did not give the police consent to search
    B. The search is unlawful because the police did not have a search warrant
    C. The search is unlawful because the police did not advise Roger that he had the right to refuse to give consent
    D. The search is legal because Roger's actions manifested his intention to give consent
    E. The search is lawful because police don't need a search warrant to search a garage, only a house

13. The police have suspicion that George has stolen property in his house. They wait until they see George leave home to go to work, and then they knock on the front door. Helen, George's wife, answers the door. The police ask her for consent to search the house. Helen says that she will not give consent unless her husband says that it is okay. The police tell Helen that they have talked with George and he said it was okay to let them into the house. Helen then gives them consent to search, and the police find the stolen property. Concerning this search, it can be said that it is:
    A. Lawful because a wife can consent to a search of the marital premises
    B. Lawful if Helen and her husband were still married and not separated or divorced
    C. Unlawful because a wife cannot consent for the husband
    D. Unlawful because the police lied to Helen and her consent was not voluntary
    E. Unlawful because the police did not have a search warrant

14. The police stop Ted for speeding. They issue Ted a warning and advise him that he is free to go. The police then ask Ted if they can search his car to make certain that he does not have any illegal weapons in the car. Ted says "Sure, go ahead and look, I don't have any guns in the car." The police search and find a marijuana joint in the ashtray. This search is:
    A. Lawful because once Ted gave consent, the police could look anywhere in the car that firearms could be hidden and arrest him if they found other contraband
    B. Lawful under the moveable vehicle exception to the requirement that police officers have a search warrant
    C. Unlawful because the police were looking for guns, not drugs
    D. Unlawful because the police did not warn Ted that he could be arrested if they found contraband other than drugs
    E. Unlawful because the police did not have a search warrant

15. The police stop Larry for speeding. They issue Larry a written warning and tell him that he is free to go. The police then ask Larry for permission to search the car for illegal drugs. Larry says "Okay." The police begin to search, but when they start to open the trunk of the car, Larry says, "Stop! I withdraw my consent to search." Police continue to search and find a sawed-off shotgun in the trunk of Larry's car. This search is:
    A. Lawful because Larry freely gave consent to search the car
    B. Lawful, but only if the police told Larry he had a right to refuse to consent to a search
    C. Unlawful because the police told Larry they were looking for drugs and found a gun
    D. Unlawful because the gun was found after Larry withdrew his consent
    E. Unlawful because the police did not have probable cause to believe that there was any contraband in the car

16. The police go to Jack's house to request consent to search the premises. Jack is not home. Which of the following people can consent to a search of Jack's house?
    A. Jack's mother-in-law, who lives with Jack
    B. Jack's twin brother, Harold, who lives next door
    C. Jack's next door neighbor, who has a key to Jack's house
    D. Jack's boss from his place of employment
    E. Jack's wife who lives with Jack in the house

17. Todd is standing by the back door of the high school smoking a cigarette. Officer Williams approaches Todd and asks Todd if he can look in Todd's book bag. Todd refuses to let Officer Williams look into his book bag. Officer Williams rips the book bag out of Todd's hands and dumps the contents on the ground. Among the items that fall out is a small bag of marijuana. This search was:
    A. Lawful, because Todd gave consent to search
    B. Lawful because Todd is a juvenile and has no right to refuse the request
    C. Lawful because the search occurred on school grounds
    D. Unlawful because the search occurred without consent
    E. Unlawful, unless Todd had a prior conviction for a drug offense

18. The police go to John's house to ask for consent to search for cocaine. They knock at the door and John answers. The police ask for consent and John says, "Do I have to let you guys come in?" The police tell John if he does not let them come in they will get a search warrant, tear his house apart and call the local TV station to come out and film the whole procedure. John then agrees to allow the police to search. The police do not find any illegal drugs in John's house. This search is:
    A. Lawful because John gave consent
    B. Lawful because the police overcame John's reluctance only by telling him truthfully what they would do if he refused
    C. Lawful because no illegal drugs were found and so there was no illegal seizure
    D. Unlawful because the police coerced John to agree to give consent

Essay Questions:

1. Why should police, armed with a valid warrant, try to obtain consent before searching a residence?

2. Why do experts say that, before you ask a person for consent to search, you should identify who they are and what relationship they have to the property where you want to search?

3. Should police have to tell a subject that they have the right to refuse a request to search before asking for consent? What would be the result of adding this requirement to the law of consent searches?

Harris v. United States (1968)

Horton v. California (1990)

Illinois v. Andreas (1983)

Michigan v. Long (1983)

Minnesota v. Dickerson (1993)

New York v. Class (1986)

Texas v. Brown (1983)

United States v. Jacobsen (1984)

United States v. Johns (1985)

United States v. Santana (1976)

Warden v. Hayden (1967)

OUTLINE

I. Requirements of the plain view doctrine
- A. Officer is in a place where he has a legal right to be
    - a. Effecting an Arrest or Search Incident to Arrest
    - b. Stop and Frisk
    - c. Executing a search warrant
    - d. Making controlled deliveries
    - e. Pursuing a fleeing suspect
    - f. Responding to an emergency
- B. Officer must not intrude on a person's reasonable expectation of privacy
- C. The incriminating character of the object to be seized must be immediately apparent to the officer
    - a. Probable cause
    - b. Electronic or mechanical aids
    - c. Shifting position
    - d. Closer examination of items
- D. The discovery of the item of evidence by the officer need **not** be inadvertent.

II. "Plain touch" or "plain feel"

REVIEW QUESTIONS

Fill in the blank:

1. In order for a police officer to make a seizure of an object in plain view, the officer must be in a __________________ where he has a legal right to be.

2. In order to seize an object in plain view, the object must be _____________________ to the officer as evidence or contraband when he views it.

3. The intrusion and observation need not be accidental or ____________________.

4. Plain view is an exception to the requirement in the _____________Amendment to the United States Constitution that officers must have a search warrant.

5. There is no reasonable expectation of privacy if contraband is displayed in plain view in a _________________ place where anyone walking by could see it.

6. The plain view doctrine does not give police a _______________ to look anywhere they want or to seize anything that they may desire.

7. In order for a seizure under the plain view doctrine to be lawful, the officer must be in a place where they have a ________________ right to be.

8. An officer making a valid arrest can seize items of evidence or contraband that are in _________________ at the location where the arrest is being made.

9. During a Terry frisk of an automobile for weapons, police can use the plain view doctrine to seize ___________________ that they may observe during the search.

10. Officers making a protective sweep of premises prior to searching with a valid search warrant can seize items of evidence and contraband that are in ________________.

11. In a controlled delivery, police arrange for the delivery of a package known to contain __________________ and then, upon delivery, arrest the recipient for its illegal possession.

12. Police that are in hot ____________________ of a suspect may seize items of evidence that are in plain view.

13. Exigent circumstances means ______________________.

14. Once the exigent circumstances are over, the justification for the _______________ is over.

15. Police must be able to determine that the object in plain view is contraband without moving it or ______________________ it.

16. Seizure of an item in plain view is warranted if the officer has __________________ to believe that it is contraband.

17. In determining probable cause, officers may use their training and _______________ to interpret what they see.

18. Police officers may use flashlights at night to ________________ their ability to see items in plain view.

19. Sometimes the ___________________of a container can be determined from its outward appearance, distinctive configuration, or shape.

20. Under the plain view doctrine, the discovery of the evidence by the officer need not be _______________________ or inadvertent.

True or false:

1. _____A search under the plain view doctrine requires that police officers have a search warrant.

2. _____To seize an item in plain view, the officer must be in a place where they have a legal right to be.

3. _____To seize an item under the plain view doctrine, an officer must have probable cause to believe that the item is evidence or contraband.

4. _____The plain view doctrine gives police the authority to go any where they want to go and seize anything that they want to seize.

5. _____The plain view exception to the requirement that police officers have a search warrant was written into the United States Constitution by those who wrote the Bill of Rights.

6. _____The plain view doctrine does not enlarge the permissible scope of a search conducted incidental to a lawful arrest.

7. _____Under the plain view doctrine, the discovery of an item of contraband by the officer must be inadvertent.

8. _____A police officer who is in a place where they have a legal right to be could pick up a book and read it to determine if its contents were evidence of a crime.

9. _____Officers can use their training and experience to help them determine that what they are looking at is evidence or contraband.

10. _____Exigent circumstances may justify an intrusion into a building where normally a search warrant would be required to enter.

11. _____Exigent circumstances will justify an entry without a search warrant, even if it is not a real emergency, but one that is contrived by the police.

12. _____There is no "crime scene exception" to the requirement that police must have a search warrant.

13. _____With regard to exigent circumstances, when the emergency is over the right to intrude on the premises is over as well.

14. _____Under the plain view doctrine, the incriminating nature of the item must be readily apparent to the police officers.

15. _____The plain view exception applies only to observations made by the police in public places.

16. _____A police officer could use binoculars to improve their ability to see items in plain view.

17. _____Opening containers to see what is inside is justified by the plain view exception.

18. _____Observations of persons' activities in a public restroom may violate their reasonable expectation of privacy, even though the officer could observe them from a place where they had a legal right to be.

19. _____ "Plain feel" is an extension of the concept of plain view.

20. _____An officer in an apartment investigating a noise complaint would be justified in picking up a television set to record its serial number so that they could later check to determine if it was stolen, because the TV was in plain view when they saw it.

Multiple Choice:

1. The plain view exception to the requirement that police officers have a search warrant requires all of the following **except:**
   A. The officer must be in a place where they have a legal right to be
   B. The item to be seized must be readily apparent as evidence or contraband
   C. The officer can use a flashlight to improve his view
   D. The discovery of the item must be inadvertent
   E. The observation not violate the person's reasonable expectation of privacy

2. Officer Martin walks by Oscar's car, which is parked in a public parking lot. Officer Martin sees a bag of marijuana on the front seat of the car. Based on the plain view doctrine, it can be said that:
   A. Seizure of the marijuana without a search warrant would be illegal
   B. Officer Martin will have to be able to testify that he can recognize marijuana when he sees it
   C. Officer Martin can seize the marijuana only if Oscar consents to the search
   D. Plain view would allow a seizure only if the marijuana was outside the car
   E. Officer Martin must be absolutely certain that what he sees is marijuana in order to seize it

3. Officer Martin walks by Tom's car, which is parked in the high school parking lot. He opens the passenger side door and reaches under the front seat, where he finds a bag of marijuana under the front seat. Under the plain view doctrine, it can be said that this seizure is:
   A. Lawful, because the bag of marijuana was in plain view after he pulled it out from under the seat
   B. Lawful, because there is no reasonable expectation of privacy in a school parking lot
   C. Unlawful, because Officer Martin did not have a search warrant
   D. Unlawful, because the marijuana was not in plain view from outside the car
   E. Unlawful, because Tom did not consent to the search

4. Officer Robbins is called to a domestic at 123 Elm Street. While talking to the victim in the living room, Officer Robbins observes a marijuana plant growing in a pot in the kitchen. Under the principles of plain view, Officer Robbins may:
   A. Do nothing, because the call to 123 Elm Street dealt only with a domestic
   B. Ask the victim about the marijuana and, if she confirms it is marijuana, seize it
   C. Break off a leaf from the plant and take it to the police department for a test
   D. Seize the marijuana plant without a search warrant
   E. Return to the station and prepare an application to obtain a search warrant based on his observations

5. The police obtain a search warrant for Mary's house for cocaine. While executing the search warrant, a police officer looks in a closet and finds a sawed-off shotgun. The gun will be:
   A. Admissible if it was immediately apparent as contraband
   B. Admissible only if the police found cocaine, too
   C. Admissible, but only if Mary gave consent to search
   D. Inadmissible, as the gun was not listed on the search warrant
   E. Inadmissible because police did not have authority to look under the bed

6. Officer Robbins finds Marty sleeping in his car. Officer Robbins orders Marty out of the car and, as Marty exits, Officer Robbins observes what he recognizes as the butt of a handgun under the front seat. Officer Robbins removes the handgun and charges Marty with its illegal possession. If admissible at trial, it will be because of the exception known as:
   A. Plain view
   B. Moveable vehicle
   C. Consent
   D. Inventory
   E. Search incident to a lawful arrest

7. Officer Thomas responds to a report of shots fired and finds Todd standing over his wife with a handgun in his hand. Officer Thomas seizes the gun and calls for an ambulance. The ambulance arrives and takes the wife to the hospital. Police arrest Todd and take him to jail. Police then search the house for evidence related to the crime and find illegal drugs in the basement. If the drugs are offered into evidence at trial against Todd, they most likely will be:
   A. Admissible under the plain view exception
   B. Admissible under the crime scene search exception
   C. Admissible, as officers were on the premises due to exigent circumstances
   D. Inadmissible because police did not have a search warrant
   E. Inadmissible because Todd did not consent to the search

8. Police are serving a search warrant for cocaine at 123 Elm Street. While inside the house, officers observe a glass jug containing a clear liquid. The officers who see it sitting on the table do not know what it is. While they continue to search the house for cocaine, a DEA chemist arrives and identifies the liquid by marking it on the bottle as a precursor chemical for phencyclidine. Police seize the bottle as evidence. If admitted at trial as evidence, it will most likely be:
   A. Admissible as the product of a plain view seizure
   B. Inadmissible because it was not listed in the search warrant
   C. Inadmissible because it was not readily apparent to the first officer who saw it
   D. Inadmissible because the DEA chemist was not there when officers began to search
   E. Inadmissible because the owner of the house had a reasonable expectation of privacy regarding the glass jug

9. Officer Zettler stops Tad based on reasonable suspicion and frisks him based on a reasonable concern for his own safety. In Tad's jacket pocket, Officer Zettler feels what his training and experience has taught him is a packet of crack cocaine. Officer Zettler seizes the crack as evidence. If admitted at trial, it will be because of the exception to the search warrant requirement known as:
   A. stop and frisk
   B. plain view
   C. plain feel
   D. moveable vehicle exception

10. Officer Martin is serving a search warrant for cocaine at 123 Elm Street. While searching in the bedroom, Officer Martin opens a closet door and finds a sawed-off shotgun, which is illegal to possess under state law. Officer Martin can:
    A. Seize the shotgun if it was readily apparent to him to be contraband
    B. Leave the shotgun and go obtain a search warrant, then return and seize it
    C. Not seize the shotgun, because his search warrant was only for cocaine
    D. Seize the shotgun, but he can not use it in evidence in a criminal prosecution
    E. Close the door and continue searching for cocaine

11. Officer Harrison makes a traffic stop on a vehicle for speeding. When he approaches the stopped vehicle, he uses his flashlight to illuminate the inside of the car. Under the passenger seat he observes a handle of a revolver. Officer Harrison orders the driver out of the car, searches under the passenger seat and finds a revolver. With regard to this search and seizure, it can be said that it is:
    A. Legal if the traffic stop was legal
    B. Illegal, because Officer Harrison could not immediately recognize what he saw as a handgun
    C. Illegal if carrying a handgun in the passenger compartment of a motor vehicle is illegal
    D. Illegal, even though he ordered the driver out of the car before seizing the handgun

12. In question 11 above, Officer Harrison's use of the flashlight was:
    A. Legal as a means of improving his view
    B. Legal if it was at night, but illegal if during the daylight
    C. Illegal as it intruded on the driver's expectation of privacy
    D. Illegal, unless Officer Harrison uses a flashlight in all traffic stops that he makes
    E. Illegal if the handgun would not be in plain view without it

13. Drug Agent Smith rents a bucket truck and uses the hydraulic bucket while parked on the street to look into Oscar's third story windows. Agent Smith observes Oscar placing rocks of cocaine into plastic bags. If Agent Smith attempts to seize the drugs on a plain view theory, the evidence most likely will be:
    A. Admitted, because Agent Smith was in a place where he had a legal right to be
    B. Admitted, because Agent Smith could tell based upon his training and experience that the object was cocaine
    C. Admitted, because possession of cocaine is a crime
    D. Suppressed, because Oscar did not give his consent
    E. Suppressed, because it was a violation of Oscar's reasonable expectation of privacy

14. Officer Johnson is walking through a public parking lot. Officer Johnson looks into Todd's parked car and sees something on the passenger seat. Officer Johnson cannot tell what the object is from that vantage point. Officer Johnson walks around the car to the passenger side, looks through the window, and sees that the item is a marijuana cigarette. If seized under a plain view theory, the evidence most likely will be:
   A. Admitted because Officer Johnson is a police officer
   B. Admitted because, once Officer Johnson adjusted his position, she could see what was readily apparent to her to be contraband
   C. Suppressed because Officer Johnson could not tell what the object was when she first observed it
   D. Suppressed because Officer Johnson was not 100% sure that the item seized was marijuana until after the crime lab tested it
   E. Suppressed because no other illegal drugs were found in the car

15. Officer Sims is walking by Jack's car that is parked in a public parking lot. Officer Sims looks into the car and sees something on the console between the front seats. Officer Sims has some suspicion that the item may be illegal drugs. He opens the unlocked car door, picks up the object from the console, and immediately recognizes it as an illegal drug. If offered into evidence under the plain view exception that officers have a search warrant, the drugs most likely will be:
   A. Admitted, because when Officer Sims examined the object he knew that it was illegal drugs
   B. Admitted, because Officer Sims had some suspicion to believe that the object he saw on the console might be illegal drugs
   C. Admitted because the car was unlocked, and there is no expectation of privacy in an unlocked car
   D. Suppressed, because Officer Sims did not have probable cause to believe the object was illegal drugs until after he entered the car
   E. Suppressed, because Officer Sims did not have Jack's consent to enter the car

16. Officer Wilson makes a traffic stop on Helen's car because she was speeding. Officer Wilson approaches Helen's stopped car and observes a checkbook on the passenger seat. Officer Wilson reaches through the open passenger door window and picks up the checkbook. When he opens the checkbook, he sees that it is for a checking account for a person named Sue Jones. Officer Wilson checks with his dispatcher and determines that the checkbook is stolen. If offered into evidence under the plain view doctrine, the checkbook most likely will be:
   A. Admitted because it was readily apparent to be a checkbook
   B. Admitted because the passenger side car window was rolled down
   C. Admitted because there is no expectation of privacy in a stolen checkbook
   D. Suppressed because Officer Wilson did not have probable cause to seize it
   E. Suppressed because Sue Jones was not there to identify her checkbook

17. Package Express handles thousands of packages each day. One day a package falls off a conveyor belt and breaks open. A package handler observes a white power leaking from the package. He sets the package aside and notifies his supervisor, who advises the manager, who calls the police. Police arrive and fieldtest the white powder, which was positive for cocaine. Police had Package Express reseal the package and arranged for a controlled delivery. If offered into evidence under a plain view exception, the drugs most likely will be:
    A. Admitted, because such an inspection would be legal
    B. Suppressed, because the police were using Package Express as their agent
    C. Suppressed, because the field test was an invasion of a reasonable expectation of privacy
    D. Suppressed, because Package Express did not have a search warrant when they opened the package
    E. Suppressed, because the shipper of the package had intended only Package Express and not the police to observe the contents of the package

18. The United States Supreme Court decision that established the "plain feel" doctrine is:
    A. Horton v. California
    B. Minnesota v. Dickerson
    C. New York v. Class
    D. Coolidge v. New Hampshire
    E. Michigan v. Long

19. The police suspect that Harry is counterfeiting twenty-dollar bills in his basement. They do not have sufficient evidence to establish probable cause. The police go to Harry's house and knock on the door. Harry invites the officers into his house. While sitting in the living room talking with Harry, officers observe a sheet of twenty-dollar bills in a wastebasket in the foyer. This is an example of:
    A. The plain touch doctrine
    B. The plain feel doctrine
    C. Eminent domain
    D. The good faith exception
    E. The plain view doctrine

Essay Questions:

1. Should the state courts require "inadvertence" as a requirement for plain view? Why or why not?

2. Night vision scopes allow officers to see events in total darkness as if it were daylight. Should an officer be allowed to use a night vision scope to enhance his vision in a plain view context?

3. Oscar builds a ten-foot high fence in front of his house so no one can see his house from the street. Officer Jones places a ten-foot high ladder on the street in from of Oscar's house and from that vantage point sees a marijuana plant in Oscar's front yard. If seized under the plain view exception, what result? Why?

4. Officers Smith and Todd respond to a domestic call. Upon arrival they hear shouting and sounds of a struggle inside the residence. Their knocks at the front door go unanswered. Officers rush into the house and find the couple standing in the living room. In plain view in the kitchen is a marijuana plant. Can the officers seize the marijuana plant? Why?

Chambers v. Maroney (1970)

Michigan v. Thomas (1982)

Pennsylvania v. Labron (1996)

California v. Carney (1985)

Coolidge v. New Hampshire (1971)

United States v. Ross (1982)

United States v. Johns (1985)

United States v. Di Re (1948)

Wyoming v. Houghton (1999)

California v. Acevedo (1991)

United States v. Chadwick (1977)

Illinois v. Lafayette (1983)

South Dakota v. Opperman (1976)

Colorado v. Bertine (1987)

Florida v. Wells (1990)

Cardwell v. Lewis (1974)

United States v. Knotts (1983)

United States v. Karo (1984)

<u>OUTLINE</u>

I. The Carroll Doctrine
- A. Probable Cause
- B. Delay in Search
- C. Exigent Circumstances
- D. Entry on private premises
- E. Scope of Search
    1. Search of entire vehicle
    2. Search of containers found in vehicle

3. Search of containers not found in vehicle
4. Other container searches

II. Impoundment and Inventory of vehicles
- A. Impoundment
- B. Inventory
  1. Standard procedure
  2. Scope
  3. Time

III. Expectation of privacy
- A. Electronic beepers
- B. Searches by dogs

REVIEW QUESTIONS

Fill in the blank:

1. The courts have held that a person has a ____________________ expectation of privacy in a motor vehicle than they do in their home.

2. A search under the Carroll Doctrine requires that the officer have knowledge of facts and circumstances that would give them ____________________ to believe that there is contraband in the vehicle.

3. Under the Carroll Doctrine, a police officer with probable cause to search a moveable vehicle does not have to go to a judge to obtain a ____________________.

4. The amount of probable cause necessary to search under the Carroll Doctrine is the same amount as required to obtain a valid ____________________ from a judge.

5. If police have probable cause to believe that the vehicle is stolen, they can seize the ____________________ itself under the Carroll Doctrine.

6. If possible, warrantless searches under the Carroll Doctrine should be done ____________________ at the scene where the vehicle is stopped.

7. Police may search a vehicle under the Carroll Doctrine after it has been towed and ____________________.

8. A state court interpreting a state constitution may impose ____________________ standards on law enforcement officers than does the United States Supreme Court.

9. Exigent circumstances may justify the warrantless search of a vehicle even if the vehicle is not ____________________.

10. If officers have justification to stop and search a vehicle on the public highway, they may follow that vehicle onto ____________________ property and search it there under the Carroll Doctrine.

11. A car without an engine would not be __________________ and therefore could not be searched under the Carroll Doctrine.

12. The ______________________ of a warrantless search defines where the officers may look within that vehicle.

13. If officers have probable cause to believe that there are illegal drugs in a motor vehicle, then they would be authorized in searching the __________________car.

14. If police have probable cause to believe that contraband is in a suitcase being transported in a motor vehicle, police could search the _______________, but not the whole car.

15. Officers may not conduct body searches of ________________ of a motor vehicle under the Carroll Doctrine.

16. Police with probable cause to search an automobile for cocaine could search anywhere in the car that cocaine could be _________________.

17. Under the Carroll Doctrine, if officers have probable cause and the vehicle is moveable, the officers may search the car without a __________________.

18. A ________________ is an inspection and recording of the condition and contents of a motor vehicle before it is towed or impounded by the police.

19. In order for items found during an inventory of a vehicle to be admitted into evidence, police must show that they have a written policy requiring inventories and a regular ____________________ of conducting them.

20. If an officer conducting an inventory of a vehicle observes an item that is readily apparent to them to be contraband, it could be seized and used as evidence under the ___________________ Doctrine.

True or False:

1. _____Under the Carroll Doctrine, police can search any moveable vehicle anytime that they want to.

2. _____The amount of evidence necessary to justify a search under the Carroll Doctrine is less than that required to obtain a search warrant.

3. _____A trained police dog makes an alert on Oscar's parked car indicating that there are illegal drugs inside. Police can search Oscar's car without a search warrant.

4. _____The Carroll Doctrine applies to all moveable vehicles, not just automobiles.

5. _____The Carroll Doctrine could be used to justify the search of a mobile home being pulled down the highway by a truck if there was sufficient probable cause.

6. _____Police could tow a vehicle to an impound lot and then search it there under the Carroll Doctrine, if they had probable cause to do so.

7. _____Exigent circumstances may justify the warrantless search of a vehicle, even though the vehicle is not movable.

8. _____When law enforcement officers would be justified in stopping and search a vehicle on the public highway under the Carroll Doctrine, they may also follow the vehicle onto private property and legally search it there.

9. _____The scope of the search under the Carroll Doctrine is defined by the nature of the object to be seized.

10. _____Officers may conduct body searches of occupants of a vehicle under the Carroll Doctrine.

11. _____Police officers with justification to search a car may search passenger belongings found in the car that are capable of containing the object of the search.

12. _____When officers have probable cause to search a container in a vehicle, they may search that container, but not the entire vehicle.

13. _____Police with probable cause to search a vehicle for cocaine could search the entire vehicle and any containers in the vehicle that could conceal the cocaine.

14. _____Under the Carroll Doctrine, police with probable cause could search a movable semi-tractor trailer without a search warrant.

15. _____The Carroll Doctrine gives police the authority to search movable vehicles without probable cause.

16. _____The Carroll Doctrine permits the search of a moveable container in a public place without a search warrant.

17. _____If a police officer has probable cause to search a particular container in a motor vehicle, they may search that container, but not the whole vehicle.

18. _____Police need probable cause to inventory a vehicle before impoundment.

19. _____Police can stop a vehicle on the roadway, search the vehicle and, if they find illegal drugs, use those illegal drugs to establish probable cause to justify the search of the vehicle.

20. _____Police can search a movable vehicle without a search warrant, even if they have no suspicion that there are illegal drugs in the car.

Multiple Choice:

1. In order to search under the Carroll Doctrine, police need:
   - A. Reasonable suspicion
   - B. Probable cause
   - C. Any movable vehicle
   - D. A passenger car

2. The Carroll Doctrine could be applied to:
   - A. Houses
   - B. Apartments
   - C. Cabins
   - D. Storage units
   - E. Airplanes

3. The amount of probable cause required under the Carroll Doctrine is:
   - A. The same as required to get a search warrant
   - B. Less than the amount necessary to obtain a search warrant
   - C. More than the amount necessary to obtain a search warrant
   - D. More or less, depending upon the size of the vehicle involved
   - E. More or less, depending upon the nature of the item to be seized

4. Officer Jones stops a car for speeding. While Officer Jones is writing the citation for speeding, Officer Smith arrives with her drug dog, Viking. Viking walks around the stopped vehicle and alerts, signaling that there are illegal drugs in the car. On these facts, Officer Jones may:
   - A. Ask the driver to wait while he obtains a search warrant
   - B. Search the entire car for illegal drugs
   - C. Ask for permission to search and search the car only if the driver consents
   - D. Do nothing, because only Viking smelled the drugs
   - E. Detain the driver while sending Viking to obtain a search warrant

5. In question 4 above, Officer Jones can take the action that he does because:
   - A. The driver gave permission to search the car
   - B. Viking is a dog
   - C. Viking's reactions gave Officer Jones probable cause
   - D. He and Officer Smith can overpower the driver of the car
   - E. Viking gave permission for the search

6. In order to legally seize contraband found during the inventory of a vehicle about to be towed, police must have:
   A. Probable cause
   B. A written departmental policy
   C. Consent to search from the driver
   D. A practice of inventorying cars about to be towed
   E. A written departmental policy and consent to search from the driver

7. The decision of the United States Supreme Court that established the authority of police to make warrantless searches of movable vehicles based on probable cause was:
   A. Mapp v. Ohio
   B. Terry v. Ohio
   C. Carroll v. United States
   D. Gideon v. Wainwright
   E. Michigan v. Long

8. In order to justify a warrantless search of a motor home based upon probable cause to believe that there were illegal drugs inside the motor home, police have to show that:
   A. The motor home was not occupied
   B. The motor home was not be used as a habitation
   C. The motor home was licensed as a vehicle
   D. The motor home was movable
   E. The motor home was parked in a public place

9. Officer Wilson stops Oscar's car for speeding. When she approaches the car to ask Oscar for his driver's license, Oscar rolls down his car window and a cloud of marijuana smoke rolls out. Under the Carroll Doctrine, Officer Wilson may:
   A. Search the entire car, including any containers that may contain marijuana
   B. Search only the area immediately surrounding the driver
   C. Report her suspicions to her sergeant, who may then issue a search warrant
   D. Issue Oscar a citation for speeding and send him on his way, because she did not see him smoking marijuana
   E. Detain Oscar until a search warrant can be obtained from a judge

10. Officer Johnson has probable cause to believe that Howard has cocaine concealed on his motorcycle. Officer Johnson follows Howard for a short while to allow back-up units to get into position. Before Officer Johnson can stop Howard on the roadway, he pulls his motorcycle into a friend's driveway. Under the Carroll Doctrine, Officer Johnson may:
    A. Keep Howard under surveillance and stop him when he pulls back onto the highway
    B. Enter the property and search the motorcycle
    C. Keep Howard under surveillance while other units obtain a search warrant
    D. While standing on the public roadway, beacon to Howard and ask him to bring his motorcycle down to the street so that he can take a look at it. When he does, he then can search the motorcycle.

11. The amount of evidence in a vehicle containing contraband necessary to justify a search under the Carroll Doctrine is:
    A. Reasonable suspicion
    B. Proof beyond a reasonable doubt
    C. Probable cause
    D. Clear and convincing evidence
    E. Absolute proof

12. Police on patrol find a rental truck stuck in the snow along a rural highway. The driver indicates that he has called a tow truck to pull him out of the snow. While the officers await the arrival of the tow truck, a canine unit arrives and checks the truck. The drug dog alerts on the rental truck. Police may:
    A. Search the truck, because the dog's alert gave them probable cause to search a movable vehicle
    B. Wait until the tow truck comes and pulls the truck out of the snow, and search it once it is again movable
    C. Not search the vehicle without a warrant, because it is not moving
    D. Not search the truck, because the Carroll Doctrine applies only to automobiles
    E. Leave the truck and go and get a search warrant

13. Oscar is pulling his boat on a trailer behind his car. Police stop Oscar for speeding and, while officers write him a citation, a drug dog alerts on Oscar's boat trailer. Police may:
    A. Search the car but not the boat trailer, because the car is the movable vehicle
    B. Search the boat and trailer without a search warrant
    C. Search the trailer, but not the boat without a search warrant
    D. Search the boat, but not the trailer without a search warrant
    E. Search the car, boat and trailer without a search warrant

14. The police have probable cause to believe that Oscar is bringing cocaine into town in his car. They stop Oscar's car. The police may search:
    A. Anywhere in the car that cocaine may be concealed
    B. Only the passenger compartment of the vehicle
    C. Only the trunk of the car
    D. Only Oscar and any containers that he has inside the car
    E. Only the passenger compartment and any containers in the passenger compartment where cocaine could be concealed

15. The police have probable cause to believe that Alice is bringing marijuana into the state in her car. They stop Alice on the highway. It can be said that:
    A. The police can search only Alice's car
    B. The police cannot search Alice's car
    C. The police can search Alice's car, any containers in the car, and all of the passengers in the car
    D. The police can search Alice's car, any containers in the car that could conceal marijuana, and any belongings of the passenger's that could contain marijuana

16. Police place a beeper inside a container of a precursor chemical used to make illegal drugs. They then follow the car of the person who buys the chemicals to a clandestine drug lab. This would be:
    A. A legal use of a electronic beeper
    B. Legal only if the driver of the car had prior notice that the chemicals contained the beeper
    C. Legal only if a Title III warrant were obtained before installing the beeper
    D. An illegal invasion of the privacy of the purchaser of the chemicals
    E. An illegal search and seizure prohibited by the Fourth Amendment to the United States Constitution

17. Police stop Oscar for speeding. While the officer writes the citation, a drug dog is brought to the scene. The drug dog walks around the outside of the car and makes no indications of a "hit." Officers then remove the passenger from the car and allow the dog to enter the car. The dog then alerts to illegal drugs in the glove compartment of the car. If offered into evidence at trial, the drugs would most likely be:
    A. Admitted into evidence under the Carroll Doctrine
    B. Admitted into evidence, but only if the drug dog could be shown to be reliable
    C. Suppressed, because the dog entered the car and searched without probable cause
    D. Suppressed, because the vehicle was not moving at the time it was searched
    E. Suppressed, because the driver has an expectation of privacy in his car

18. Officer Hawkins stops a car with four male juveniles in it. Officer Hawkins searches the car and finds a marijuana cigarette in the ashtray. The driver of the car admits to Officer Hawkins that the "joint" is his. If introduced into evidence at trial, the marijuana will most likely be:
    A. Admitted, because possession of marijuana is a crime
    B. Admitted, because the driver admitted that it was his marijuana
    C. Admitted, because it was found in a search of a movable vehicle
    D. Admitted, because four juveniles in a car creates sufficient suspicion for a stop and search
    E. Suppressed, because the search was illegal

19. Officer Smith observes Harold carrying a suitcase. Officer Smith has probable cause to believe that the suitcase contains heroin. Officer Smith follows Harold and stops him just as he is about to enter a taxi. Officer Smith searches the suitcase and finds heroin. If offered into evidence at trial, the heroin most likely will be:
    A. Admitted, because possession of heroin is illegal
    B. Admitted, because the suitcase was movable
    C. Admitted, because the suitcase was about to enter a movable vehicle
    D. Suppressed, because the search and seizure was illegal
    E. Suppressed, because a taxi is not a movable vehicle under the Carroll Doctrine

20. In order to make a lawful search under the Carroll Doctrine, a police officer needs:
    A. Probable cause
    B. Reasonable suspicion
    C. A movable vehicle
    D. A search warrant
    E. Probable cause and a movable vehicle.

Essay Questions:

1. What is necessary for a proper inventory?

2. How does the alert of trained drug dog allow for the search of an automobile?

3. How does the amount of probable cause required to obtain a valid search warrant compare to the amount necessary to search a vehicle under Carroll v. United States?

4. Martin is homeless and living in his car. Police develop probable cause that Martin has stolen property in his car. What steps must officers take to search Martin's mobile residence?

5. Is a car in a police impound lot still a moveable vehicle? Should police have to obtain a search warrant to search a car they hold in their own impound lot? Why or why not?

CHAPTER 11
OPEN FIELDS AND ABANDONED PROPERTY

KEY TERMS AND CONCEPTS

ABANDONED PROPERTY – Property whose owner has voluntarily discarded, left behind, or otherwise relinquished his or her interest in the property with no further reasonable expectation of privacy in the property.

CURTILAGE – The area around the house protected by the Fourth Amendment requirement that officers have a search warrant. Courts deal with the issue on a case by case basis and no set boundary is set by law.

HOUSES – "Houses" includes homes, whether owned, rented, or leased and any other place in which a person is staying or living, permanently or temporarily.

OPEN FIELDS – Any area outside the home which is not curtilage.

PLAIN VIEW DOCTRINE – Doctrine which states that "if police are lawfully in a position from which they view an object, if its incriminating character is apparent, and if the officers have a lawful right of access to the object, they may seize it without a warrant."

REASONABLE EXPECTATION OF PRIVACY – The area of privacy the court has determined that society is willing to accept as reasonable.

SEARCH – A government action where an expectation of privacy that society is prepared to consider reasonable has been infringed.

KEY CASES

Hester v. United States (1924)

Oliver v. United States (1984)

United States v. Dunn (1987)

California v. Ciraolo (1986)

Dow Chemical Co. v. United States (1986)

Florida v. Riley (1989)

Abel v. United States (1960)

Smith v. Ohio (1990)

California v. Greenwood (1988)

OUTLINE

I. Hester v. United States
II. Open Fields
  A. Determination of curtilage
    1. Residential yard
    2. Fences
    3. Distance from the dwelling
    4. Multiple-occupancy dwellings
    5. Garages
    6. Other outbuildings
    7. Unoccupied tracts
  B. Reasonable expectations of privacy
  C. Plain view, open fields, and observations into constitutionally protected areas
    1. Aerial observations
    2. Driveways and other means of access to dwellings
III. Abandoned Property
  A. Indications of intent to abandon property
    1. Premises
    2. Objects
    3. Motor vehicles
  B. Lawfulness of police behavior
  C. Reasonable expectation of privacy in the property

REVIEW QUESTIONS

Fill in the blank:

1. Under Hester v. United States, there is no ___________________of privacy in the open fields.

2. The difficulty with the open fields doctrine is to differentiate the _________________ from the open fields.

3. The protection of the ___________ Amendment to the United States Constitution extends to apartments, dormitory rooms, motel rooms, and hospital rooms, as well as to traditional residences.

4. The ___________________ is the name applied to the grounds immediately adjacent to the house.

5. The backyard of a house has repeatedly been held to be within the ______________ and therefore a protected area under the United States Constitution.

6. If a residential yard is open to the public and the owner takes no steps to protect it from observation, it may not qualify for the ________________ afforded by the United States Constitution.

7. If the area around a house is surrounded by a fence, then this area would be defined as the ____________________.

8. Erecting fences around land that is in the open fields will not give it the ____________________ guaranteed by the United States Constitution.

9. Some courts have used a rule that the curtilage ends approximately ____________ feet from the dwelling.

10. Multiple-occupancy dwellings are treated ___________________ than single family homes in determining the curtilage.

11. Porches and fire escapes in multiple family dwellings would fall within the ___________________ for a multiple-occupancy dwelling.

12. Garages are usually held to be part of the __________________.

13. Whether an outbuilding is protected by the Fourth Amendment would depend in part upon its ________________ from the residence.

14. An unoccupied remote tract of land would be held to be __________________.

15. Under Oliver v. United States, even the placement of _________________ signs will not extend protection to the open fields.

16. Police flying over a home could make lawful observations of activities inside the ___________________ of the residence.

17. If officers gather information while standing in a public _______________, the officers will not violate a citizen's expectation of privacy.

18. An officer's observation from a public place may give them the _________________ necessary to obtain a search warrant.

19. There is no expectation of ________________ in abandoned property.

20. When a person leaves _________________ at the curb for pickup, they no longer have an expectation of privacy in that material.

True or False:

1. _____There is no expectation of privacy in the open fields.

2. _____The curtilage of a residence is protected by the Fourth Amendment to the United States Constitution.

3. _____Leaving property unattended for a long period of time is a strong indication of intention to abandon the property.

4. _____The curtilage is the area six feet around the outside of the house.

5. _____The curtilage of every house has exactly the same dimensions.

6. _____A field with a fence around it and a no trespassing sign would be protected by the Fourth Amendment.

7. _____There is no expectation of privacy in abandoned property.

8. _____The backyard of a residence is within the curtilage of the house.

9. _____A person who places garbage at the curb for pickup has abandoned that property.

10. _____Outbuildings are always held to be within the curtilage of the residence.

11. _____A house under construction would be still within the open fields.

12. _____Police cannot fly over a house and make observations within the curtilage.

13. _____A small patch of ground within a cornfield that was surrounded by a fence would be protected by the Fourth Amendment to the United States Constitution.

14. _____Observations by a police officer standing on public property will be lawful even if they are of a protected area of a residence.

15. _____Officer Jones is walking down a sidewalk in front of Oscar's house when he through a plate glass window sees a marijuana plant growing in a pot in the living room. Officer Jones must obtain a search warrant to seize the marijuana plant.

16. ____ In determining whether property is abandoned, courts will look at the owner's intent.

17. _____Property left behind in a motel room when you check out is abandoned property.

18. _____Denial of ownership is a factor that can be used to establish that property is abandoned.

19. _____Discarding property in reaction to unlawful actions by law enforcement officers is not abandonment of the property.

20. _____A police officer may search the open fields without probable cause or a search warrant.

Multiple Choice:

1. Which of the following could police **not** search without a search warrant?
   A. A cornfield
   B. An abandoned automobile
   C. An attached garage of a residence
   D. An outbuilding outside the curtilage
   E. Garbage left at the curb for pick up

2. The decision of the United States Supreme Court that established that there is no expectation of privacy in the open fields is:
   A. Mapp v. Ohio
   B. Miranda v. Arizona
   C. Carroll v. United States
   D. Gideon v. Wainwright
   E. Hester v. United States

3. In order for the police to search the open fields, they must have:
   A. A search warrant
   B. An arrest warrant
   C. Probable cause
   D. Reasonable suspicion
   E. There is no requirement to search the open fields

4. Protected living quarters under the Fourth Amendment to the United States Constitution would not include:
   A. A single-family residence
   B. An apartment
   C. A dormitory room
   D. A hotel room
   E. Abandoned property

5. Which of the following areas of a business would be protected by the Fourth Amendment to the United States Constitution?
   A. The parking lot that is open to the public
   B. The lobby of an office building open to the public
   C. The sales floor of a retail store
   D. The produce section of a grocery store
   E. The manager's office of an appliance store

6. The enclosed area of ground immediately adjacent to a dwelling house is called the:
   A. Curtilage
   B. Out lot
   C. Escarpment
   D. Residue
   E. Boutique

7. Martin's residence has a backyard that is adjacent to the local school. Students cut through the yard daily on their way to and from school. There is no fence, and the students have worn a path that is used by neighbors and strangers alike to access the school property from the street. On these facts, it can be said that Martin's backyard is:
   A. Part of the curtilage and protected by the Fourth Amendment
   B. Part of the curtilage, but not protected by the Fourth Amendment
   C. Not part of the curtilage, because the yard is open to public use
   D. Not part of the curtilage, because Martin does not have no trespassing signs posted
   E. Not part of the curtilage, because Martin lives next door to the school

8. Oscar grows corn on a forty-acre field on his farm. In the middle of one of the cornfields, Martin erects an eight-foot high fence and posts no trespassing signs on the fence. Inside the fenced area, Oscar grows marijuana. Concerning this small fenced-in area, it can be said that it is:
   A. Part of the curtilage, because Oscar fenced it
   B. Part of the curtilage, because Oscar posted no trespassing signs
   C. Part of the curtilage, because Oscar deemed that it be so
   D. Not part of the curtilage, because it is in the open fields
   E. Not part of the curtilage, because Oscar is growing marijuana there

9. A *per se* rule for establishing the area of the curtilage of a house would be that:
   A. All houses have a curtilage that extends 75 feet from the back door
   B. Various factors, such as whether the area is fenced or posted must be considered
   C. The intent of the property owner to have privacy must control
   D. Each case must be judged on its own individual merits

10. Tom's garage is attached to his single family home. It can be said that it is:
    A. Part of the curtilage of the residence
    B. Part of the curtilage so long as he keeps the door closed
    C. Part of the curtilage, but only if he has it posted with no trespassing signs
    D. Not part of the curtilage, because it is a garage and not part of the living area
    E. Not part of the curtilage, unless he uses it for sleeping rather than parking his car

11. Jack lives in a rural area. The area behind is house is fenced in with an eight-foot high fence that runs some 200 feet behind the house. The fence is made of oak boards. There are no gaps or holes in the fence and only one gate that is always kept closed and locked. Concerning the area within the fence, it can be said that it is:
    A. Within the curtilage because it is fenced in
    B. Within the curtilage because it is adjacent to the house
    C. Outside the curtilage because it is so very large
    D. Outside the curtilage because it is in a rural area
    E. Outside the curtilage because it was not posted with no trespassing signs

12. Maurice owns a very expensive home in a fashionable suburb. Behind his house, he has a greenhouse where he grows orchids and marijuana. The greenhouse is 200 feet from the residence and is not surrounded by a fence. Concerning the greenhouse, it can be said that it is:
    A. Protected by the Fourth Amendment, because it is in the curtilage
    B. Protected by the Fourth Amendment, because Maurice is very rich
    C. Protected by the Fourth Amendment because Maurice is growing orchids, which are legal to possess
    D. Not protected by the Fourth Amendment because Maurice is growing marijuana, which is illegal to possess
    E. Not protected, because the greenhouse is outside the curtilage and within the open fields

13. Some distance from Mary's house, she owns a small tract of land that is unoccupied, uncultivated and remote from her residence. Mary is attached to this land because it has been in her family for many years, passed down from one generation to another. Concerning this tract of land, it can be said that it is:
    A. Within the curtilage
    B. Within the curtilage if Mary wants it to be so
    C. Within the curtilage, because it historically has been Mary's private property
    D. Outside the curtilage, because it is remote, uncultivated and undeveloped
    E. Outside the curtilage, because Mary has not posted it with a sign that said "curtilage"

14. Drug Agent Smith flies over Oscar's house and observes marijuana growing inside a fenced area adjacent to the house. Based on his training and experience, Agent Smith has probable cause to believe that Oscar is growing marijuana in his backyard. Agent Smith lands his airplane, locates a judge, and obtains a search warrant. If offered into evidence at trial, the marijuana will be:
    A. Admitted, because Agent Smith's observations from the plane were lawful
    B. Admitted, because there is no expectation of privacy when growing marijuana
    C. Suppressed, because the marijuana was observed within the curtilage
    D. Suppressed, because flying over Oscar's house violated his expectation of privacy
    E. Suppressed, because Officer Smith did not submit a sample of the marijuana with his application for a search warrant

15. Officer Jones is looking for a missing child. He goes to the residence at 123 Elm Street, walks up the sidewalk onto the front porch, and knocks on the door to ask the residents at that address if they have seen the child. While standing on the front porch, Officer Jones smells what his training and experience cause him to believe is coming from an illegal clandestine drug lab. Further investigation and surveillance lead to a successful application for a search warrant that yields illegal drugs, lab apparatuses, and precursor chemicals. If offered into evidence at trial, the drugs will be:
    A. Admitted, because the manufacture of illegal drugs is illegal
    B. Admitted, because Officer Jones's observations while standing on the front porch were lawful
    C. Suppressed, because Officer Jones violated the Fourth Amendment by coming onto the porch
    D. Suppressed, because Officer Jones smelled the illegal drugs cooking and did not actually see them
    E. Suppressed, because Officer Jones's initial entrance onto the property was to look for a missing child and that is all he was authorized to do there

16. Officer Robbins is walking down Main Street when he sees what his training and experience have taught him is a marijuana plant growing inside Molly's second floor apartment. Officer Robbins is standing on the public sidewalk, and he can clearly see the marijuana plant inside Molly's apartment through the front window. On these facts, Officer Robbins may:
    A. Immediately enter Molly's apartment and seize the plant because it was in plain view
    B. Keep Molly's house under surveillance until he has proof beyond a reasonable doubt that she is selling marijuana
    C. Ignore the plant, because it is within a legally protected area where Molly has an expectation of privacy
    D. Use his observations as probable cause to obtain a search warrant and then seize the marijuana plant
    E. Contact Molly's landlord and have her evicted

17. Officer Martin sees Oscar standing on a street corner. Officer Martin pulls up in his marked police car and gets out of the car to say hello to Oscar. As soon as Oscar sees Officer Martin, he starts to run away. Officer Martin chases Oscar on foot to investigate what he is up to. As Oscar runs, he throws down a small plastic bag. Officer Martin scoops up the small plastic bag and catches up with Oscar. Investigation later reveals that the small plastic bag contained cocaine. If offered into evidence at trial against Oscar, the cocaine will be:
    A. Admitted, because possession of cocaine is a crime
    B. Admitted, because Oscar abandoned the bag when he threw it down
    C. Admitted, because Oscar has been convicted before of dealing illegal drugs
    D. Suppressed, because Oscar retained an expectation of privacy over the plastic bag
    E. Suppressed, because Officer Martin did not have a search warrant when he started to chase Oscar

18. Police think that Ralph is dealing child pornography. Police want to check Ralph's garbage to see if they can find evidence of child pornography. Ralph puts his garbage in a big plastic garbage can that he leaves outside his back door. On Wednesdays, the city's waste disposal department stops in front of Ralph's house, and a sanitation employee goes onto the property, empties the garbage into the city truck, and returns the can to its location beside Ralph's back door. On these facts, police may:
    A. Enter Ralph's property at any time and seize his garbage in his garbage can
    B. Enter Ralph's property and seize the garbage, but only on Wednesdays
    C. Wait until the city employees place the garbage onto their truck and then seize it
    D. Wait until the city garbage truck dumps its load at the landfill, and then look for Ralph's garbage there
    E. Not seize Ralph's garbage, because Ralph has a perpetual expectation of privacy in his trash

19. Larry rents a one-room apartment in an apartment building on a month-to-month basis. Larry has no lease, but simply pays his landlord by the 5th of each month for the current month's rent. Larry leaves his apartment without notice, taking most of his clothing and possessions with him. He does not pay the rent for three months. Police arrive looking for Larry in connection with a murder. The landlord unlocks Larry's apartment and police search without a search warrant, finding evidence that links Larry to the murder. If offered into evidence at trial, the evidence will most likely be:
    A. Admitted, because Larry is a murderer
    B. Admitted, because any property he left behind was abandoned
    C. Suppressed, because police did not have a search warrant
    D. Suppressed, because police did not have his permission to enter his apartment
    E. Suppressed, because the landlord could not consent to a search of the apartment

20. Tom forges several checks and obtains $10,000 in the process. Fearful that police are looking for him, Tom checks out of his motel room and leaves town quickly. Police go to the motel room and get the maid to open the door to the room that Tom had occupied. In the room in the wastebasket, they find blank checks linking Tom to the crime. On these facts, if offered into evidence at trial, the checks will most likely be:
   - A. Admitted as the fruits of the crime
   - B. Admitted, because Tom abandoned them when he checked out of the motel
   - C. Suppressed, because police did not have a search warrant for the motel room
   - D. Suppressed, because the hotel maid and not the hotel manager opened the door for the police
   - *E.* Suppressed, because Tom has a continuing expectation of privacy in the room that he rented at the motel

Essay Questions:

1. Would it be helpful if there was one uniform definition of curtilage that was applicable in all jurisdictions and in all situations? What should that definition be?

2. Should police be able to enter a constitutionally protected area without a search warrant or exigent circumstances when they observe contraband in plain view?

3. How much evidence of criminal activity do the police need to search an area that is within the open fields?

4. Should the police need a search warrant to search an area of private property that is bounded by a ten-foot fence and clearly marked with no trespassing signs, even if it is within the open fields?

5. Todd shoots his wife as she is getting out of his car at her work. Todd rushes home and buries the murder weapon in a hole he dug the night before in his back yard. Todd goes into the house and hides in the attic. Police detectives arrive at Todd's house to advise him of his wife's death and to question him about his whereabouts at the time of the murder. Police knock on the front and back doors without response. Seeing the activity, the next door neighbor comes out from his residence and tells the police officers about seeing Todd come home in the middle of the day and bury a gun in a hole in his backyard. Police walk with the neighbor into the neighbor's backyard and he points out the freshly dug earth in Todd's back yard.
   A. Can police borrow a shovel from the neighbor and dig up the gun?
   B. Should they leave and get a search warrant?
   C. What if the police see Todd watching them in the neighbor's backyard from an attic window? Does that create exigent circumstances?
   D. Do the police have probable cause to arrest Todd right now? If so, do they need an arrest warrant, or can they go into Todd's house and arrest him now?

CHAPTER 12
ADMISSIONS AND CONFESSIONS

KEY TERMS AND CONCEPTS

ADMISSION – A voluntary acknowledgement of the existence of certain facts. An admission is not limited to words, but can include demeanor, conduct and acts of the person.

COMPETENCY – Whether a suspect has the requisite level of comprehension to validly waive *Miranda* rights.

CONFESSION – A confession is a statement admitting or acknowledging the facts necessary to support a conviction for a crime. Whereas an admission is a partial confession to one or more facts, a confession admits to all facts necessary to prove all the elements of the crime.

CUSTODY – Custody occurs when a person would reasonably believe that they were not free to go. Normally we think of custody in terms of arrest, but a person can be in custody and not under arrest. And likewise during a stop under Terry v. Ohio the subject is not free to go, but he is not in custody.

INTERROGATION – The questioning of a suspect in custody for the purpose of obtaining a confession.

PUBLIC SAFETY EXCEPTION – The conclusion by the Supreme Court that the need for answers to questions in a situation posing a threat to the public safety outweighed the need to protect the Fifth Amendment's privilege against self-incrimination.

STATEMENT – Any oral or written declaration or assertion by a person.

VOLUNTARINESS – Whether a waiver of *Miranda* rights is voluntary depends upon the absence of police coercion.

WAIVER – The voluntary, intentional relinquishing of known rights. The waiver can be in writing, oral or by actions, such as answering questions after having been advised of your right not to do so.

KEY CASES

Rogers v. Richmond (1961)

Brown v. Mississippi (1936)

Townsend v. Sain (1963)

Colorado v. Connelly (1986)

Escobedo v. Illinois (1964)

Miranda v. Arizona (1966)

Dickerson v. United States (2000)

California v. Beheler (1983)

Stansbury v. California (1994)

Oregon v. Mathiason (1977)

Berkemer v. McCarty (1984)

Rhode Island v. Innis (1980)

South Dakota v. Neville (1983)

New York v. Quarles (1984)

Edwards v. Arizona (1981)

Minnick v. Mississippi (1990)

Michigan v. Jackson (1986)

McNeil v. Wisconsin (1991)

Arizona v. Mauro (1987)

Arizona v. Roberson (1988)

Patterson v. Illinois (1988)

Smith v. Illinois (1984)

Davis v. United States (1994)

Oregon v. Bradshaw (1983)

Oregon v. Elstad (1985)

Massiah v. United States (1964)

Brewer v. Williams (1977)

Maine v. Moulton (1985)

Michigan v. Mosley (1975)

CHAPTER OUTLINE

I. Historical background—admissibility of admissions and confessions
  A. Voluntariness
  B. Escobedo and Miranda
II. Facts and holdings of Miranda
III. Issues of Miranda
IV. Custody
  A. Focus of investigation
  B. Place of interrogation
    1. Police stations
    2. Prisons and jails
    3. Homes
    4. Places of business
    5. Stores, restaurants, and other public places
    6. Hospitals
    7. Crime scenes
  C. Investigative and traffic stops
  D. Time of interrogation
  E. Presence of other persons
  F. Arrest or restraint
  G. Police coercion or domination
  H. Psychological restraints
  I. Interview initiated by suspect
V. Interrogation
  A. Volunteered statements
  B. Clarifying questions
  C. Routine questions
  D. Spontaneous questions
  E. Questions related to public safety
  F. Confrontation of suspect with evidence
  G. Confrontation of suspect with accomplice
  H. Statements or actions of officers
  I. Interrogation by private citizens
  J. Multiple attempts at interrogation
    1. Attempts after right to silence is invoked
    2. Attempts after right to counsel is invoked
    3. Attempts after rights are waived
    4. Attempts after an unwarned admission
    5. Attempts after defendant is formally charged

REVIEW QUESTIONS

Fill in the blank:

1. A(n) ____________________ is an oral or written declaration or assertion by a person.

2. A(n) ____________________ is an oral or written statement or acknowledgement of the existence of facts that tend to incriminate the person in a crime.

3. A(n) ___________________ is a written or oral statement or acknowledgement of all of the facts necessary to prove the elements necessary to convict the person of a crime.

4. To be admissible in court, a confession must be ____________________ in that it was made without inducement, promises, threats or force being used to obtain it.

5. The United States Supreme Court decision in the case of _________________ v. Arizona is the key case in the area of confessions.

6. In determining whether a confession is voluntary, courts will look at the ___________ age of the defendant as well as their chronological age.

7. If no police coercion was used, a statement will be considered to be ______________.

8. If coercion is used by the police, the courts will examine the ____________________ to determine if the confession was voluntary.

9. Miranda v. Arizona deals with __________________ interrogation of a defendant.

10. Advising a subject of his Miranda Rights will not make a confession ________________ if promises, threats, or force are subsequently used to coerce a confession.

11. In Beckwith v. United States, the United States Supreme Court clearly held that the _________________ of the investigation test is not the standard for determining if Miranda warnings must be given.

12. Before 1964, the only test for the admissibility of a defendant's admission or confession was its ________________________.

13. The voluntariness requirement was established in _______________________, in which the Supreme Court held that a confession coerced from a defendant by means of police brutality violated due process of law.

14. Absent _____________________ conduct by the police, every confession is considered to be voluntary.

15. The procedural safeguards established by the Supreme Court to protect the privilege against self-incrimination are known as ________________________.

16. The warnings required by the Miranda case must be given before police question a person who is in ____________ or deprived of their freedom of action in any significant way.

17. In answering the question of whether there has been a seizure tantamount to arrest, the courts consider the ______________________________.

18. In _______________________, the Supreme Court held that a suspect questioned in a police station is not necessarily in custody.

19. Interrogation of a person at their place of business is usually held to be ___________ _________.

20. The *Miranda* requirements apply only if a person in custody is subjected to ________ _________.

True or false:

1. _____Police officers must advise a person of their Miranda rights before questioning during a Terry stop.

2. _____An involuntary confession can be used against the defendant if the case involves a very serious charge, like murder.

3. _____Volunteered statements sometimes occur when a person intentionally or unintentionally makes an incriminating statement in the presence of a law enforcement officer.

4. _____A Miranda warning must be given to a suspect in custody before questioning if the prosecutor wants to use the suspect's answers against him in court in a criminal prosecution.

5. _____Miranda warnings need not be given for misdemeanors and other minor offenses.

6. _____The court has held that clarifying questions are interrogation, and Miranda warnings are required.

7. _____When law enforcement officers ask questions spontaneously, impulsively, or in response to an emergency, the questions are usually held to be interrogation.

8. _____A confession can be voluntary if the police use promises and threats but not force against the suspect.

9. _____In the determination of custody, routine questioning is usually indicative of a lack of custody.

10. _____A suspect should always be given Miranda warnings prior to confrontation with evidence by a police officer.

11. _____The Miranda warning requirements apply only to custodial interrogations conducted by law enforcement officers.

12. _____Assertion of the right to counsel applies only to preliminary interrogation.

13. _____Courts find a statement involuntary if the statement is a product of police coercion, whether by force or by subtler forms of coercion, and if, in the totality of the circumstances, the statement is not the result of a person's free and rational choice.

14. _____Any questioning by police resulting in a confession, which is not the product of a free intellect, is inadmissible.

15. _____Police cannot make promises of leniency to a suspect during interrogation in an attempt to extract a confession.

16. _____If police coercion did not occur during questioning, then a statement will be considered voluntary, regardless of the suspect's mental or physical condition at the time.

17. _____Satisfaction of Miranda requirements is the only consideration in determining if a confession was voluntary.

18. _____The Supreme Court has stated that a delay of interrogation in excess of six hours after arrest constitutes a violation of due process.

19. _____Encouraging a suspect to tell the truth and telling them that they might be left "holding the bag" is a violation of due process.

20. _____Focus of investigation is a consideration in determining if a suspect must be given Miranda warnings.

Multiple Choice:

1. The U.S. Supreme Court decision that required that subjects in custody be advised of their rights prior to interrogation was:
    A. Mapp v. Ohio
    B. Terry v. Ohio
    C. Miranda v. Arizona
    D. Chimel v. California
    E. Belton v. New York

2. Police suspect that Chad committed a murder. Police invite Chad to the police station to talk. Whether police must advise Chad of his rights is dependent upon:
    A. Whether Chad is a suspect
    B. Whether Chad is the focus of the investigation
    C. Whether Chad is in custody
    D. Whether Chad is guilty of murder
    E. Whether Chad or the police ask the first question

3. Police arrest Tom for killing his wife. Police do not advise him of his Miranda rights. On the way to jail, Tom says, "The witch deserved it!" With regard to Tom's statement, it will be:
    A. Admissible, since it was not made in response to a question
    B. Admissible, because the crime involved was murder
    C. Admissible, but only if he had been advised of his rights
    D. Inadmissible, unless the statement was in writing
    E. Inadmissible, unless the statement was made under oath

4. In determining if a seizure tantamount to arrest has occurred, the courts will consider whether a __________________ person would feel free to leave.
    A. Competent
    B. Criminal
    C. Reasonable
    D. Considerate

5. Which of the following is <u>not</u> an issue that would be considered a factor when determining that a person was in custody for purposes of a Miranda warning?
    A. Focus of investigation
    B. Criminal record
    C. Place of interrogation
    D. Psychological restraints
    E. Police domination

6. Which of the following is <u>not</u> one of the guidelines for conducting a <u>second</u> custodial interrogation?
   A. Scrupulously honor the person's right to terminate questioning at the initial interrogation.
   B. Give the person complete Miranda warnings again.
   C. Allow a significant amount of time to intervene between the first and second interrogation attempts.
   D. Wait for the suspects' attorney to arrive.
   E. Do not employ any pressure to cooperate or other illegal tactics.

7. Under Miranda v. Arizona, police must give warnings to:
   A. Every person they meet
   B. Every person they question
   C. Every person they focus on as a suspect in a crime
   D. Every person they take into custody
   E. Every person in custody whom they want to question

8. Police arrest Tom and place him in a holding cell at the police department. Police do not advise Tom of his Miranda rights. Two hours later, a jail officer asks Tom if he is warm enough in his cell and Tom says, "No, I need a blanket." Because Tom has been subjected to custodial questioning without having been advised of his Miranda rights, it can be said that:
   A. Police must drop the charge against Tom and release him at once
   B. Police may have to drop the charges and release Tom if his defense attorney finds out about the incident
   C. Police may not use his answer to the question in evidence against him at trial
   D. Police may not use his response "No" but may use his response "I need a blanket," because that was more of a response than the question required
   E. Tom may raise this issue on appeal if convicted

9. Police must advise subjects in custody of their rights under Miranda before questioning. This applies to:
   A. Persons who have been stopped for a traffic ticket
   B. Witnesses giving their testimony
   C. Any suspect in custody
   D. Any Terry Stop

10. Which of the following actions by police is not held to be interrogation after a defendant's invocation of the right to counsel?
    A. Offering to explain the operation of the criminal justice system to the defendant
    B. Questioning about the ownership of an automobile parked at the crime scene
    C. Asking for date of birth
    D. Confronting the defendant with an arrest warrant and photographs of their fingerprints taken at the crime scene
    E. Calling the defendant by the nickname of the person believed to have committed the particular offense

11. In ________________________, the Court held that, after an accused has invoked the right to counsel, courts will not allow responses to further interrogation to be used to cast doubt on the clarity of the initial request itself.
    A. Patterson v. Illinois
    B. Oregon v. Bradshaw
    C. Miranda v. Arizona
    D. Oregon v. Elstad
    E. Smith v. Illinois

12. Police respond to a call of a shooting at 123 Elm Street. Upon arrival, Police find Mike standing over his wife's body with a gun lying on the floor. Mike says, " I didn't mean to kill her!" Under Miranda, Mike's statement will be:
    A. Admissible, because murder is a very serious crime
    B. Admissible, because it was not in response to police questioning
    C. Not admissible, because Mike was not yet in police custody
    D. Not admissible, because Mike was not advised of his rights
    E. Not admissible, because Mike hadn't been informed of his right to an attorney

13. In order to be valid, Miranda warnings must:
    A. Be given to the suspect in writing
    B. Be read from an official Miranda Card
    C. Be read to the suspect from the United States Supreme Court decision itself
    D. Be written or verbal, as long as it includes all of the information required by the Miranda decision
    E. Be given to the suspect in writing and read to them at the same time

14. Miranda warnings must be given to which of the following?
    A. A driver stopped for speeding who is asked if they know how fast they were going
    B. A witness to a crime
    C. A victim of an armed robbery
    D. A suspect in a burglary who is not in custody
    E. A suspect who is in jail on another charge awaiting trial

15. The questioning of a suspect in custody in order to obtain a confession is called:

A. Interview
B. Interrogation
C. Voir dire
D. Direct examination
E. Cross examination

Essay Questions:

1. Officer Robbins suspects that Oscar is buying and selling stolen TV sets but does not have probable cause. Can Officer Robbins invite Oscar to come down to the police station and talk? If Oscar comes to the police station, can Officer Robbins ask him directly if he has been buying stolen TV sets? Does Officer Robbins have to advise Oscar of his Miranda rights?

2. Courts have held that a waiver of Miranda rights must be made with understanding. How could you determine if a suspect understood the rights that you read to him?

3. Some police departments require officers give suspects written copies of the Miranda warnings and obtain written waivers. Other departments do not. What are the pro and con arguments for giving written warnings and obtaining signed waivers?

4. Police arrest Jack for murder. Police advise Jack of his Miranda rights. Police question Jack for 16 hours straight without a break. Police do not allow Jack to use the restroom, nor do they offer him food or water. Finally, Jack confesses to the murder and signs a statement, including a statement that the confession is made voluntarily and of his own free will. What arguments will Jack's attorney raise in a suppression hearing on this confession?

5. Malcolm places a bomb with a timer at the high school in locker #123. Malcolm calls police from a pay telephone and reports a bomb threat. Police rush to the pay telephone and arrest Malcolm. Without advising Malcolm of his rights under Miranda, police ask Malcolm, "Where's the bomb?" Malcolm answers, " in locker 123 at the high school." Before police can locate and deactivate the bomb, it explodes, killing a janitor at the school. Can police use Malcolm's statement against him at trial? Why?

CHAPTER 13
PRETRIAL IDENTIFICATION PROCEDURES

KEY TERMS AND CONCEPTS

CONFRONTATION – Showups and lineups and any presentation of a suspect to a victim or witness of a crime for the purpose of identifying the perpetrator of the crime.

LINEUP – An identification procedure where the suspect is displayed with a group of similar persons to see if the victim or witness can pick him out from the group.

SHOWUP – A one-on-one identification where the suspect is shown to the victim shortly after the crime has been committed to see if the victim can identify the suspect as the one who committed the crime

WAIVER – The voluntary, intentional relinquishing of known rights. The waiver can be in writing, oral or by actions, such as answering questions after having been advised of your right not to do so.

KEY CASES

Gilbert v. California (1967)

United States v. Wade (1967)

Kirby v. Illinois (1972)

Stovall v. Denno (1967)

Neil v. Biggers (1972)

Manson v. Brathwaiete (1977)

Simmons v. United States (1968)

United States v. Ash (1973)

OUTLINE

I. Introduction—definition of terms
II. Requirement of counsel—The Wade-Gilbert rule
  A. Basis of the Court's decision
  B. Waiver of right to counsel
  C. Substitute counsel
III. Guidelines for lineup identification
  A. Before the lineup

B. During the lineup
C. After the lineup

IV. Exceptions to the Wade–Gilbert rule
  A. Identifications conducted before the initiation of adversary judicial proceedings
    1. Kirby v. Illinois
    2. Stovall v. Denno
    3. Neil v. Biggers
    4. Manson v. Brathwaite
  B. Emergency identifications
  C. Preparatory steps

V. Photographic identifications

VI. Effect of an improper identification procedure

REVIEW QUESTIONS

Fill in the blank:

1. A collection of photographs shown to a witness in the hope that they can identify the suspect is called a ____________________.

2. Having the suspect stand among a small group of similar persons and having the victim attempt to identify the suspect is called a ______________________.

3. A one-on-one identification where the suspect is shown to the victim soon after the crime is called a ______________________.

4. A photographic showup would be the presentation of ______________________ photograph(s) to the victim.

5. A photographic lineup is also called a __________________________.

6. After indictment, a defendant is permitted to have their ___________________ present during a lineup.

7. The purpose of having the defense attorney present during a lineup is so that the attorney can observe the proceedings and make certain that the procedures used are ___________________ to the defendant.

8. Before conducting a line up, police should consult with the ____________________ for legal advice.

9. Promptly conducted lineups allow for the quick ___________________ of arrestees who are not identified by victims and witnesses.

10. A(n) ____________________ made as a result of a lineup will be suppressed if the lineup was suggestive.

11. In so far as possible, all of the persons in a lineup should be of the ______________ weight, height, age and race.

12. If a lineup is held to be suggestive, the out-of-court identification by the victim or witnesses will be ___________________ and not allowed into evidence at trial.

13. Showups are permitted by courts because they can be used to exonerate ________________ individuals who otherwise would be arrested and held until a lineup could be conducted.

14. The suspect's right to have an attorney at a lineup attaches to the_______________ of the criminal proceedings against him.

15. Due process requires that the totality of the circumstances surrounding an identification procedure not be overly ____________________.

16. The United States Supreme Court has suggested that the minimum number of photographs in a photo array should be _____________________.

17. The photos used in a photo array should be preserved so that they all can be introduced into ___________________ at trial.

18. A suggestive identification procedure is one that points to the __________________ that we want the witness or victim to identify.

19. Courts are concerned about the __________________ and accuracy of eyewitness identifications.

20. The key danger is that the out-of-court identification may taint the in-court identification and make it _____________________ at trial.

True or false:

1. _____A suspect in custody can be compelled to participate in a lineup.

2. _____The defense attorney must be present whenever a photo array is shown to a witness.

3. _____A showup can be conducted at any time.

4. _____Lineups should be conducted as soon as possible after the arrest of the suspect.

5. _____A photo array where the suspect's photograph is in color and all of the other photographs are black and white would be proper if all the photographs were the same size.

6. _____A photographic lineup and a photo array are two different names for the same thing.

7. _____A lineup with a male black suspect and five white males would be proper if all of the subjects were the same size and wore similar clothing.

8. _____Photo arrays are usually easier to prepare than lineups.

9. _____If a defense attorney is advised of a scheduled lineup and refuses to attend, the lineup cannot be held.

10. _____Only identical twins should be used in a lineup.

11. _____To save time, all witnesses should be shown a photo array at the same time.

12. _____If time is of the essence, police officers in uniform who are the same age, height, weight, and race as the suspect can be used in a lineup, even if the suspect is in a jail uniform.

13. _____Neither a lineup or a photo array may be conducted so that it is suggestive.

14. _____Multiple lineups involving the same suspects and witnesses are suggestive and should be avoided.

15. _____A suspect who has not been arrested, indicted or charged with a crime has no right to an attorney during a lineup.

16. _____Whether a lineup or photo array is suggestive or not, it will be judged by the court on the basis of the totality of the circumstances surrounding the identification procedure.

17. _____A one-on-one identification where a victim rides around with police after a crime to see if they can observe the perpetrator among pedestrians in the area would not be suggestive.

18. _____An identification made from a showup three days after the crime would not be admissible.

19. _____A photo array where the suspect's photograph was an 8x10 and the other photos were 4x6 would be permissible if all of the photographs were in color.

20. _____The danger is not so much that the out-of-court identification will be suppressed, but that the court will rule that the out-of-court identification so tainted the in-court identification that the court will not permit it introduced into evidence at trial.

Multiple Choice:

1. Prior to conducting a lineup, an officer should discuss it with the:
   - A. Defense attorney
   - B. Judge
   - C. Defendant
   - D. Duty officer
   - E. Prosecuting attorney

2. A group of persons presented to a victim or witnesses in the hope that the they can pick the suspect out of the group is called a:
   - A. Assembly
   - B. Cluster
   - C. Photo array
   - D. Lineup
   - E. Showup

3. A one-on-one identification where a suspect is shown to a victim shortly after a crime has occurred is called a:
   - A. Match up
   - B. Lock down
   - C. Showup
   - D. Lineup
   - E. Photo array

4. A group of photographs shown to a victim or witness in the hopes that they can identify the suspect is called:
   - A. Showup
   - B. Lineup
   - C. Line-down
   - D. Focus group
   - E. Photo array

5. A photographic lineup is also called a:
   - A. Picture show
   - B. Photo gallery
   - C. Photo array
   - D. Road trip
   - E. Ghost alley

6. The United States Supreme Court has suggested that the number of photographs in a photo array should be at least:
   - A. Two
   - B. Three
   - C. Six
   - D. Twelve

7. A photo showup would contain how many photographs?

A. One
B. Two
C. Six
D. Twelve
E. Any number the officer wants to use

8. An officer creates a photo array using black and white photocopies from a high school yearbook. Which of the following would be best for the suspect's photo?

A. A 4x5 color photo of the suspect taken six months ago
B. A black and white booking photo with his slate number across the bottom
C. A color wedding photo with his wife's picture covered with masking tape
D. A black and white photo copy of his high school yearbook picture
E. A color photo copy of his driver's license ID photo

9. Many police departments videotape the lineups that they conduct. The reason that they do this is so that they can:

A. Show the video to the city council to justify buying the camera
B. Show the court that the lineup was not suggestive
C. Show the witnesses and victim the video again later in case they can't make an identification this time
D. Prove that the defense counsel was present at the lineup
E. Have videos to show at the department holiday party

10. Officer Robbins is preparing a photo array to show to a victim, along with a photo of Tom who is a 24 year-old white male who is 5'7" and weighs 125 pounds. Tom's photo is a 4x6 color photo taken yesterday with a Polaroid camera at the jail. The best photos to use for the photo array would be:

A. 3x3
B. 2x2
C. 4x6
D. 8x10
E. 8x12

11. In question 10 above, Officer Robbins might include which photo from the list below?

A. Zach, who is an African-American male who is 5'9"
B. Al, who is a white male, aged 45
C. Sam, who is a Hispanic male who is 25
D. Sean, who is 22 year-old white male
E. Tad, who is a 16 year-old who is 5'8

12. In question 11, above the photos used should be:

A. Black and white
B. Color photos printed by computer
C. Color photos taken with a Polaroid camera
D. Color photocopies of pictures taken with a camera
E. Color photos clipped from magazines

13. Concerning the role of a defense attorney at a post indictment lineup, it is important to remember:

A. That the defense attorney must conduct the lineup
B. If the defense attorney must approve the lineup procedures
C. That the defense attorney must approve the persons in the lineup with their client
D. If the defense attorney refuses to attend the lineup, it cannot be held
E. That the defense attorney is there to observe the lineup

14. Police arrest Harvey for bank robbery. Harvey requests that police conduct a lineup for the five employees who were in the bank at the time of the robbery. Police:

A. Must conduct the lineup at the defendant's request
B. Must conduct the lineup, unless the defendant signs a waiver of this right
C. Must conduct the lineup if the defendant's attorney requests it
D. Must conduct the lineup, but the bank employees have the right not to attend
E. Do not have to conduct the lineup

15. Police should conduct lineups as soon as possible after the suspect's arrest because:

A. It will help the witnesses recognize the suspect in court
B. It will allow the prompt release of innocent arrestees
C. It will cut down on the expense of police overtime pay
D. It will result in a speedier trial for the defendant
E. It will give the prosecution evidence to use in a bond hearing

16. Police arrest Chester for robbery. Police want Chester to participate in a lineup so that victims of other robberies can identify him as the perpetrator in their crimes. It can be said that:

A. Chester can refuse to participate in a lineup
B. Chester can refuse to participate in a lineup, unless police pay him for his time
C. Chester can refuse to participate in a lineup, unless it is part of a plea bargain agreement
D. Chester cannot refuse to participate in a lineup
E. Chester cannot refuse to participate in a lineup, unless his attorney does not agree to his participation

17. If a suspect is not represented by an attorney at a lineup, it can be said that:

A. Police should obtain a waiver from the defendant before the lineup
B. Police should make certain that the lineup is conducted in a fair manner
C. The rules governing lineups do not apply because an attorney is not present
D. No lineup can be held
E. The lineup will be overly suggestive

18. Officer Martin arrests Sam for a burglary that occurred last week. Officer Martin wants to obtain a pre-trial identification of Sam by the only witness, John. Officer Martin works in a very small town, and there is only one other person in town who resembles Sam. Officer Martin should:

A. Conduct a showup of Martin with the witness at the police station
B. Conduct a lineup with only two people in it
C. Conduct a photo array instead of a lineup
D. Release Sam because he cannot obtain an identification from the witness
E. Put the witness into the cell with Sam, pretending he is a prisoner, to see if he can identify Sam as the guilty party

19. Neil v. Biggers listed factors to be considered in evaluating the likelihood of misidentification. These factors included all of the following **except:**

A. Witness's opportunity to view the criminal at the time of the crime
B. Witness's degree of attention
C. Accuracy of the witnesses prior description of the criminal
D. Length of time between the crime and the identification
E. The age of the witness

Essay Questions:

1. Police respond to an armed robbery of a convenience store. The victim gives a good description of the robber, and police put out a broadcast. Ten minutes after the robbery, an officer stops a suspect who matches the description of the robber, but the unit holding the suspect is uncertain if the person they are detaining is the robber. What should the police do?

2. Police want to conduct a lineup with a suspect, who is a 54 year-old white male weighing 250 pounds, dressed in a jail uniform that consists of orange coveralls. What should the other persons in the line up look like? Why?

3. What is the problem with showing a photo array to a group of witnesses in order to save time?

4. On what basis could a judge suppress an out-of-court identification by a witness and still allow the witness to identify the defendant in court?

5. Mildred is 74 and owns a small bakery. One night she is going out to her car in the unlit parking lot when she is accosted by a robber, who knocks her down and grabs her bank bag before running away. What factors would contribute to making an eyewitness identification of the suspect difficult?

ANSWER KEY

Chapter 1

Fill in the Blank:
1. Articles of Confederation; see p. 5
2. Bill of Rights; see p. 5
3. Marbury v. Madison; see p. 6
4. Legislative; see p. 7
5. Executive; see p. 7
6. Judicial; see p. 7
7. Bill of Attainder; see p. 11
8. Ex post facto law; see p. 11
9. Judicial Branch; see p. 11
10. Treason; see p. 12
11. First; see p. 12
12. First; see p. 12
13. Sixth; see p. 26
14. Eighth; see p. 28
15. Fourteenth; see p. 8
16. Sixth; see p. 25
17. Gideon v. Wainwright; see p. 27
18. Fourteenth; see p. 32
19. Eighth; see p. 28
20. Fifth; see p. 21

True or False:
1. F; see p. 5
2. T; see p. 8
3. T; see p. 8
4. F; see p. 9
5. F; see p. 11
6. T; see p. 19
7. T; see p. 12
8. T; see p. 14
9. T; see p. 17
10. T; see p. 18
11. T; see p. 19
12. F; see p. 21
13. T; see p. 23
14. T; see p. 25
15. F; see p. 28
16. F; see p. 28
17. T; see p. 28
18. T; see p. 31
19. T; see p. 31
20. F; see p. 34
21. T; see p. 22
22. T; see p. 24
24. F; see p. 10

Multiple Choice:
1. E; see p. 28
2. E; see p. 26
3. C; see p. 27
4. A; see p. 14
5. C; see p. 18
6. D; see p. 19
7. B; see p. 17
8. C; see p. 24
9. A; see p. 12
10. B; see p. 19
11. E; see p. 8
12. D; see p. 20
13. B; see p. 19
14. D; see p. 28
15. C; see p. 25
16. D; see p. 28
17. C; see p. 25
18. C; see p. 27
19. A; see p. 26
20. D; see p. 8
21. E; see p. 22
22. A; see p. 31
23. E; see p. 32

CHAPTER 2

Fill in the Blank:

1. District Court; 43
2. Circuit Court of Appeals; 44
3. Supreme Court Answer; 45
4. Limited Jurisdiction; 46
5. Complaint; 47
6. Affidavit; 50
7. Initial Appearance; 51
8. Probable Cause; 51
9. Probable Cause; 51
10. Indictment; 53
11. Grand Jury; 53
12. Bench Trial; 70
13. Count of an offense; 56
14. More than on offense; 56
15. Prosecutorial Discretion; 56
16. *Nolo contendere*; 59
17. Plea bargaining; 62
18. Motion; 63
19. Discovery; 64
20. Batson v. Kentucky; 71

True or False:

1. T; 62
2. T; 62
3. T; 43
4. T; 44
5. F; 44
6. F; 46
7. T; 46
8. T; 50
9. T; 51
10. T; 53
11. T; 56
12. T; 52
13. T; 58
14. T; 60
15. T; 63
16. T; 44
17. F; 67
18. T; 70
19. F; 71
20. F; 75

Multiple Choice:

1. C; 76
2. B; 70
3. C; 73
4. C; 44
5. C; 47
6. E; 50
7. D; 51
8. E; 53
9. B; 56
10. D; 57
11. C; 65
12. A; 64
13. D; 71
14. A; 69
15. D; 70
16. C; 74
17. C; 78
18. D; 47
19. E; 44
20. D; 45

CHAPTER 3

Fill in the Blank:
1. Weeks v. United States; 92
2. Mapp v. Ohio; 92
3. New Federalism; 94
4. Supreme Court; 93
5. Admissible; 92
6. Evidence; 98
7. Independent; 98
8. Criminal; 92
9. Fourth; 92
10. Police; 92
11. Suit; 95
12. Immunity; 96
13. Constitution; 94
14. Nix. V. Williams; 98
15. Leon v. United States; 101
16. Search warrant; 101
17. Unconstitutional; 103
18. Evidence; 92
19. People; 106
20. Reasonable; 92

True or False:
1. T; 92
2. F; 92
3. T; 92
4. T; 92
5. F; 95
6. T; 92
7. F; 92
8. F; 101
9. T; 45
10. T; 93
11. T; 92
12. T; 94
13. F; 110
14. F; 110
15. T; 113
16. F; 113
17. T; 102
18 .T; 93
19. T; 92
20. T; 92

Multiple Choice:
1. B; 92
2. C; 92
3. E; 92
4. D; 92
5. D; 92
6. E; 92
7. B; 92
8. B; 103
9. E; 103
10. A; 99
11. D; 101
12. C; 92
13. B; 104
14. C; 92
15. B; 110
16. C; 104
17. E; 92
18. C; 121
19. B; 99
20. C; 94

CHAPTER 4

Fill in the Blank:	*True or False*:	*Multiple Choice*:
1. Fourth; 154	1. F; 173	1. B; 154
2. Arrest; 154	2. T; 168	2. B; 196
3. Arrest warrant; 160	3. T; 168	3. B; 157
4. Submission; 154	4. F; 168	4. A; 168
5. Body; 155	5. F; 179	5. B; 159
6. Authority; 155	6. F; 168	6. B; 184
7. Intent; 156	7. T; 160	7. A; 185
8. Detention; 157	8. T; 169	8. D; 185
9. Probable cause; 161	9. T; 172	9. D; 180
10. *De facto* arrest; 154	10. T; 198	10. A; 179
11. Possession; 175	11. T; 177	11. A; 185
12. Complaint; 160	12. T; 179	12. B; 190
13. Summons; 164	13. F; 179	13. A; 185
14. Misdemeanor; 168	14. T; 180	14. D; 160
15. Probable cause; 154	15. T; 181	15. E; 190
16. Felony; 168	16. T; 179	16. C; 190
17. Pursuit; 177	17. T; 180	17. D; 185
18. Garner v. Tennessee; 180	18. T; 183	18. A; 168
19. Payton v. New York; 183	19. T; 184	19. A; 181
20. Ker v. Illinois; 196	20. T; 185	20. B; 183

CHAPTER 5

Fill in the Blank:	*True or False*:	*Multiple Choice*:
1. Fourth; 210	1. F; 251	1. D; 244
2. Judge; 212	2. F; 212	2. E; 244
3. Probable cause; 213	3. T; 212	3. E; 246
4. Stale; 216	4. T; 271	4. D; 212
5. Person; 217	5. F; 219	5. B; 213
6. Contraband; 217	6. F; 219	6. E; 216
7. Fruits of the crime; 217	7. T; 219	7. B; 218
8. Evidence; 213	8. F; 219	8. B; 214
9. Instrumentalities; 216	9. T; 219	9. C; 210
10. Particularity; 219	10. T; 226	10. B; 214
11. Affidavit; 213	11. T; 226	
12. Secure; 226	12. T; 227	
13. Anticipatory; 227	13. T; 230	
14. Announce; 235	14. T; 235	
15. Area; 243	15. T; 235	
16. Lockers; 252	16. T; 235	
17. Warrant; 256	17. F; 219	
18. Inadmissible; 271	18. T; 244	
19. Judicial; 260	19. T; 245	
20. Administrative; 247	20. T; 246	

CHAPTER 6

Fill in the Blank:
1. Suspicion; 296
2. Terry v. Ohio; 297
3. criminal; 292
4. police officer; 311
5. Weapons; 311
6. Experience; 296
7. Less; 286
8. Arrest; 311
9. Reasonable; 307
10. Force; 304
11. Car; 311
12. Stop; 314
13. Stop; 292
14. Constitutional; 319
15. Racial profiling; 319
16. Unlawful; 319
17. Reasonable; 331
18. Not given; 331
19. Safety; 304
20. Judge; 314

True or False:
1. F; 314
2. F; 292
3. T; 292
4. T; 292
5. T; 307
6. F; 292
7. F; 292
8. T; 292
9. F; 292
10. T; 292
11. T; 292
12. T; 292
13. T; 292
14. T; 292
15. F; 286
16. T; 299
17. F; 299
18. T; 299
19. T; 304
20. T; 304

Multiple Choice:
1. B; 287
2. E; 292
3. C; 311
4. E; 314
5. A; 292
6. E; 292
7. C; 330
8. D; 330
9. E; 330
10. D; 311
11. C; 302
12. B; 315

CHAPTER 7

Fill in the Blank:
1. Arrest; 348
2. Lawful; 348
3. Warrant; 348
4. Evidence; 348
5. Not; 348
6. Record; 348
7. Frisk; 348
8. Container; 355
9. Area; 358
10. Limited; 358
11. Container; 353
12. Crime; 348
13. Object; 355
14. Sweep; 358
15. Plain View; 358
16. Probable Cause; 347

True or False:
1. F; 347
2. T; 360
3. F; 360
4. T; 355
5. T; 348
6. T; 353
7. T; 353
8. T; 355
9. F; 347
10. T; 355
11. F; 357
12. T; 358
13. F; 358
14. F; 358
15. T; 353
16. T; 364
17. T; 366
18. F; 358
19. F; 348
20. F; 355

Multiple Choice:
1. B; 355
2. A; 358
3. B; 347
4. E; 358
5. D; 353
6. E; 348
7. A; 355
8. C; 355
9. E; 355
10. E; 352

CHAPTER 8

Fill in the Blank:	*True or False*:	*Multiple Choice*:
1. Voluntarily; 376	1. T; 376	1. D; 394
2. Warrant; 376	2. F; 377	2. D; 396
3. Probable cause; 376	3. F; 382	3. C; 396
4. Promises; 377	4. F; 381	4. D; 377
5. Voluntarily; 377	5. T; 382	5. D; 381
6. Force; 377	6. T; 377	6. E; 377
7. Consent; 381	7. T; 376	7. A; 392
8. Before; 378	8. F; 383	8. A; 397
9. Consent; 380	9. F; 385	9. A; 378
10. Consent; 381	10. T; 387	10. C; 390
11. Suppressed; 378	11. T; 387	11. A; 394
12. Search; 388	12. F; 388	12. D; 385
13. Plain view; 388	13. T; 391	13. D; 380
14. Reasonableness; 388	14. T; 388	14. A; 390
15. Consent; 389	15. T; 392	15. D; 391
16. Container; 390	16. T; 392	16. E; 392
17. Jointly; 392	17. F; 395	17. D; 377
18. Judge; 384	18. F; 396	18. D; 378
19. Child; 399	19. F; 397	
20. Voluntarily; 392	20. T; 397	

CHAPTER 9

Fill in the Blank:

1. Place; 413
2. Immediately apparent; 413
3. Inadvertent; 413
4. Fourth; 412
5. Public; 412
6. License; 413
7. Legal; 413
8. Plain view; 414
9. Evidence; 414
10. Plain view; 414
11. Contraband; 415
12. Pursuit; 416
13. Emergency; 417
14. Search; 417
15. Manipulating; 430
16. Probable cause; 413
17. Experience; 422
18. Enhance; 424
19. Contents; 426
20. Accidental; 413

True or False:

1. F; 413
2. T; 412
3. T; 413
4. F; 413
5. F; 412
6. T; 414
7. F; 413
8. F; 413
9. T; 422
10. T; 417
11. F; 417
12. T; 418
13. T; 417
14. T; 413
15. F; 413
16. T; 424
17. F; 413
18. T; 419
19. T; 430
20. F; 430

Multiple Choice:

1. D; 413
2. B; 413
3. D; 413
4. D; 413
5. A; 432
6. A; 413
7. D; 430
8. A; 415
9. C; 430
10. A; 420
11. A; 423
12. A; 423
13. E; 413
14. B; 424
15. D; 420
16. D; 420
17. A; 415
18. B; 412
19. E; 412

CHAPTER 10

Fill in the Blank:
1. Lesser; 442
2. Probable cause; 442
3. Search warrant; 443
4. Search warrant; 443
5. Vehicle; 454
6. Immediately; 443
7. Impounded; 454
8. Stricter; 456
9. Moveable; 444
10. Private; 447
11. Moveable; 447
12. Scope; 448
13. Whole; 448
14. Suitcase; 450
15. Passengers; 450
16. Concealed; 448
17. Search warrant; 442
18. Inventory; 454
19. Practice; 454
20. Plain view; 454

True or False:
1. T; 442
2. F; 442
3. T; 443
4. T; 442
5. T; 445
6. T; 454
7. T; 444
8. T; 447
9. T; 448
10. F; 450
11. T; 450
12. T; 450
13. T; 448
14. T; 442
15. F; 442
16. F; 420
17. T; 450
18. F; 454
19. F; 443
20. F; 443

Multiple Choice:
1. B; 443
2. E; 442
3. A; 443
4. B; 463
5. C; 463
6. E; 456
7. C; 442
8. D; 442
9. A; 443
10. B; 447
11. C; 443
12. A; 463
13. B; 463
14. A; 443
15. D; 443
16. A; 462
17. C; 463
18. E; 443
19. D; 443
20. E; 442

CHAPTER 11

Fill in the Blank:	*True or False*:	*Multiple Choice*:
1. Expectation; 476	1. T; 476	1. C; 481
2. Curtilage; 477	2. T; 477	2. E; 476
3. Fourth; 477	3. T; 491	3. E; 476
4. Curtilage; 477	4. F; 477	4. E; 477
5. Curtilage; 478	5. F; 477	5. E; 494
6. Protection; 478	6. F; 478	6. A; 477
7. Curtilage; 478	7. T; 491	7. C; 487
8. Protection; 478	8. T; 477	8. D; 478
9. 75; 479	9. T; 500	9. A; 479
10. Differently; 480	10. F; 481	10. A; 481
11. Curtilage; 481	11. F; 482	11. A; 478
12. Curtilage; 481	12. F; 486	12. E; 482
13. Distance; 481	13. F; 478	13. D; 482
14. Open fields; 482	14. F; 485	14. A; 486
15. No trespassing; 482	15. T; 485	15. B; 485
16. Curtilage; 486	16. T; 491	16. D; 485
17. Place; 485	17. T; 491	17. B; 491
18. Probable cause; 485	18. T; 498	18. C; 500
19. Privacy; 491	19. T; 492	19. B; 491
20. Garbage; 500	20. T; 476	20. B; 493

CHAPTER 12

Fill in the Blank:
1. Statement; 514
2. Admission; 514
3. Confession; 514
4. Voluntary; 514
5. Miranda; 514
6. Mental; 516
7. Voluntary; 528
8. Totality of the circumstances; 517
9. Custodial; 518
10. Admissible; 528
11. Focus; 522
12. Custody; 514
13. Brown v. Mississippi; 515
14. Coercive; 517
15. Miranda Warnings; 520
16. Custody; 521
17. Totality of the circumstances; 522
18. Oregon v. Mathiason; 523
19. Noncustodial; 525
20. Initiates; 530

True or False:
1. F; 527
2. F; 514
3. T; 531
4. T; 519
5. F; 561
6. F; 532
7. F; 533
8. F; 514
9. T; 532
10. F; 535
11. T; 536
12. F; 539
13. T; 517
14. T; 515
15. F; 516
16. T; 517
17. F; 519
18. T; 516
19. F; 516
20. T; 522

Multiple Choice:
1. C; 514
2. C; 523
3. A; 531
4. C; 522
5. B; 521
6. D; 538
7. E; 518
8. C; 522
9. C; 514
10. C; 542
11. E; 543
12. B; 531
13. D; 550
14. E; 519
15. B; 514

CHAPTER 13

Fill in the Blank:

1. Photo array; 580
2. Lineup; 580
3. Showup; 580
4. One; 580
5. Photo array; 580
6. Attorney; 584
7. Fair; 584
8. Prosecutor; 583
9. Release; 583
10. Identification; 592
11. Same; 583
12. Suppressed; 592
13. Innocent; 589
14. Commencement; 589
15. Suggestive; 599
16. 6; 598
17. Evidence; 598
18. Suspect; 586
19. Reliability; 580
20. Inadmissible; 581

True or False:

1. T; 583
2. F; 597
3. F; 590
4. T; 583
5. F; 598
6. T; 580
7. F; 583
8. T; 598
9. F; 583
10. F; 583
11. F; 598
12. F; 583
13. T; 592
14. T; 588
15. T; 580
16. T; 602
17. T; 590
18. F; 593
19. F; 597
20. T; 580

Multiple Choice:

1. E; 583
2. D; 580
3. C; 580
4. E; 580
5. C; 580
6. C; 583
7. A; 580
8. D; 598
9. B; 586
10. C; 598
11. D; 598
12. C; 598
13. E; 583
14. E; 583
15. B; 583
16. D; 583
17. B; 583
18. C; 598
19. E; 580

Notes

Notes

Notes

Notes